Jihad: A Struggle or Terrorism?

Second Edition, 2013

SPECIAL EDITION TO SUPPORT **HILLARY CLINTON** and
SARAH PALIN TO BE NOMINATED THE NEXT USA
PRESIDENTIAL CANDIDATES (see page 103-104)

Jihad: A Struggle or Terrorism?

First Edition, 2002

Second Edition, 2013

Mumbai and Boston bombings, London

Attack, and Syrian Civil War are included

in this second edition

Illustration and cover design by author

ISBN 978-0-9892988-2-7

Acknowledgment

To novie, zaki, zaka, lia and fiki thanks for your support and patience.

A special acknowledgment is attributed to:

AuthorHouse of Bloomington IN,
createspace.com and **amazon.com**

What to read first in this book

For your convenience, you may skip Chapter Three and read it later. This Chapter is portraying the world situation around 2001 as a background of various violent conditions around the globe.

How to use the Qor'an reference

The numbers inside the brackets are the sequential numbers of Surah and verse in the Qor'an. If we find the text of "--it should be done with good manners (not the violence and terrorism, **16:125**)" it does mean we may check the original text and/or its translation in Surah 16 verse 125. The sequential numbers of Surah are enclosed in the Appendix.

Table of Contents

September 11, 2001 is the sorrow
for the innocence
and
a tragedy for the humanity
no doubt
everyone does agree
who does have
the right to splash the blood
regardless who did

nobody can find the single phrase
in any book
to justify the mass destruction
of the innocence people
a single question
why it happened
the answer is vary
this book is trying to find out
the possible answer from the past history
and
normative sources

arb 0902

Foreword for Second Edition

It has been idle for 11 years since the first edition; and now the second edition of "**Jihad: A Struggle or Terrorism?**" is ready to read. During this long period, some stunning incidents such as **Mumbai** and **Boston** bombings happened. Therefore these two terror incidents are included in this second edition.

Without the hard work of **1stBookLibrary**/ AuthorHouse; the first and monumental edition of this book is impossible; therefore all staffs deserved my appreciation and thankfulness.

This book is simple if compared to my other book -- about a part of American History especially the Cuban Missile Crisis-- "**John F. Kennedy's Nuclear War**" ISBN 978-0-9892988-0-3 which was originally 560-page long before being "compressed" into 434 pages, published in May 2013. Anyway, a simple explanation in this book would be convenient for the busy readers like you. As of this second edition (2013) is available; and then the first edition (2003) should have not been printed and/or circulated anymore.

Thank you for your attention to this second edition.

Cleveland, OH USA
July 2013
abahry@hotmail.com

Terminology

Abyssinia	ancient Ethiopia, a country in Africa, the initial destination of Moslems migration
Ahlul-Hilli wal-Aqdi	the House of Experts, the board of clerics assigned as the House of Representative
Al-Kholafaa'ur-Raashedeen	the four successors of Mohammad in the Islamic administration, they were Abu Bakr, Omar bin Khattab, Osman bin Affan, and Ali bin Abu Taleb.
Arkaanul-Iman	the six basic principles of Islamic faith
Arkaanul-Islam	five Islamic principles
Asbaabun-Nozool	the context of a verse revelation
Bae'atur-Ridwan	The Pledge of Readiness of 628 AD, an assembly to make the pledge to fight the people of Mecca if Osman bin Affan was killed during his visit to Mecca
Companions	the friends of Mohammad
Darul-Harb	the country of enemy
Darul-Islam	the Moslem country
Divide et impera	divide and rule, a method of dividing a nation to occupy later, this method was used by the colonialists
Dunya	everything related to the present life and hedonism

Fiqh	the Islamic law
Hadiths, Sunnah or Decree	all Mohammad's words, actions, answers and decrees related to the Islamic rules and practices
Istinbaat	proper discussion and library research by the experts of Islamic law to conclude a certain case
Ijma	the consensus on the Islamic law
Istinja	the way to clean body from the material dirt such as urine, feces, menstrual discharge, etc or non-material dirt such as the condition after wet dream or marital relationship, or spiritual dirt because the polytheists or atheists do not recognize God who created them
Kabah	the ancient building built by Abraham and Ismail in Mecca as the central of religious activity and uniformity of prayer direction
Maliky	a school of Islamic thoughts especially in the realm of Islamic law during the classic period of the development of Islam, the other schools are Hanafy, Shafie and Hanbaly
Mustalah hadith	the knowledge to know and differentiate between a fake hadith and an original one

Najs	dirty according to Islamic law, najs maybe something is "clean" and even sterile but if it contain a substance of ham, urine etc. it is considered najs
Okhowwah	Moslem brotherhood based on the religion no matter the native and origin
Osol-fiqh	the method to conclude the law
People of the Holy Scripture	the people who practiced the teaching of the previous prophets
Pesantren	a method of study in a small group where the interaction between student and tutor is very high
Qesas	the equal punishment
Qiyas	the jurisprudence
Qor'an	the divine sentences revealed by God to Mohammad the Prophet conveyed by Gabriel the Angel, the composition and meaning came from God no interference therein
Salatul-hajat	the midnight prayer to ask for the divine guidance
Shahadah	the pledge to acknowledge God is One and Only Lord, and Mohammad is the Messenger of God
Sunnah or the Hadith	is all Mohammad's words, actions, answers and decrees related to the Islamic rules and practices.

Surah	Chapter
Tafsier ijtehaad	the translation of Qor'an based on the knowledge and logic after fulfilling the requirements for translation
Tafsier manqool	a translation of a verse in Qor'an based on another verse or translating a verse with a decree (hadith) of Mohammad
Taoqeefy	the method of compiling the Qor'an, it was not compiled based on the chronology but on a decree conveyed by Gabriel the Angel
Ummah	the Moslem society
Zabeha	the meats of slaughtered cattle prepared under the Islamic rule

Preface

> Some Qor'an verses were misunderstood not by non-Moslems only but also by Moslems themselves, because the language used in the Qor'an is quite different from the Arabic language spoken by most Arabs in Arab countries. Therefore, at the very beginning I realized that this book might be causing a controversy.

The complexity of verse has lead some misunderstandings even between the Arabs, moreover not every scholar can memorize the *Asbaabun-Nozool* or the context of verse revelation; it is very important since some famous cases can be resolved with referring to the Asbaabun-Nozool (see Chapter Four).

When Prophet Mohammad still alive, his companions used to directly ask him to resolve the problem. Today the Moslems are far away from the era of Mohammad and his companions, if there is any serious problem they should make "istinbaat" (proper discussion and library research to conclude a certain case).

The **Chapter One** of this book is highlighting Brief History of Islam, the condition of Arab peninsula before and after Islam including the struggle of power as Mohammad passed away. The severe rivalry between them has produced the small kingdoms as the inevitable outcome, then the Ottoman came as a crystallization of intent to unify the Moslem; but unfortunately Kemal Ataturk came with his secular thought to put the good beginning in a vain.

Chapter Two comes with the perspective of Islam in the modern world; there are some examples how the Moslem life is. They lived in the poverty, uneducated, bad health, under unjust government, corruptive administration, and civil war as the further outcome of the western colonialism. The detail of Soeharto and Abacha saga in the Chapter Two is to show how fragile the power is, it is obtained after a long struggle but generates a very short time result with so many victims, tears, blood and even curse. The history is harder than power, impression is sharper than bullet.

"Who terrorized whom" is a good question but the answer is miscellaneous and depends upon the different point of view. **The Chapter Three: Brief History of Violence** is dealing with historical facts and not the justification over who was wrong and who was right. The condition mentioned in the Chapter Two is very conducive for the seeds of violence to grow in any form, that's the correlation with Chapter Three. It is a matter of fact that there is almost no spot in the world free from the violence. This is the world situation before, during and shortly after the tragedy of 9/11 where the terrorists slammed two airplanes to the World Trade Centre, New York on September 11, 2001 This Chapter contains the excerpts a lot of violence in most part of the world. The detail of Afghanistan is intended to elaborate how this country never tired from the bloody conflicts since 50 years ago. It had more than 10 presidents during 29 years; it ever had 2 presidents in just the same time and had 2 Secretaries of Defense in the same time of another decade. It should have been recorded in The Book of World Record: a president ruled for only three months after assassinating 'the previous president, and then he was assassinated and replaced by another. They were Taraki, Amin, and Karmal; three presidents in a year even in a single semester of 1979!

There is no topic more popular than Jihad today. Is it a basis for the suicide bombing, hijacking and other violence? This hot question will be discussed in **Chapter Four: Understanding of Jihad,** Chapter Five and Chapter Six. It is not easy to decide which such an action is lawful or unlawful in Islam. The knowledge of Qor'an verses, Arabic, Tafsier, Hadith, Mustalah-hadith, Asbaabun-Nozool, Fiqh and Osol-fiqh should be implemented accordingly before deciding The Paradigm of Jihad.

The freedom of thought is good, but the open discussion is better. There are some misunderstood verses we will discuss in **Chapter Five**; four of them are most disputed verses since the third Moslem generation (700 AD or 100 Hijrah) to the classic era (1100 AD or 500 H) until today. Nevertheless, Prophet Mohammad gave the guideline "I left two things, if you persist on them you will be never lost forever, they are the Qor'an and the Sunnah". The Sunnah or hadith is all Mohammad's words, actions, answers and decrees related to the Islamic rules and practices.

The most four misunderstood verses are about (1) Jihad, (2) marriage, (3) People of the Holy Scripture, and (4) zabeha. This book will discuss briefly each of them, and the preliminary explanation in the previous chapters is necessary for more understanding about the disputes and the background as well.

The dispute however has its own advantage and detriment, and leads to the rise of four mainstream schools (mazaheb): Maliky, Hanafy, Shafie and Hanbaly in the classic period.

During the lifetime of Mohammad there were eight major wars, we will find out in the **Chapter Six: The Doctrine of War** why and when the wars occurred, and we will discuss the consequence of war including the truce, status of POW and ethics of war in the Islamic Law. We will also find that the Arabs in 626 AD had recognized the art of disinformation; this method had been used as a part of psychological warfare as well as the utilization of trench as a method of defense for the superiority of real war.

The important jihad in this century is to establish the Islamic schools to fight the stupidity, to build the research laboratories for the mankind welfare and to adopt the orphans from the Moslem countries around the world to prevent them from being burden for the society in the future.

The jihad is a continuous effort to invite the mankind into Islam peacefully and Qor'an in perusal periodicals. How come to teach the Qor'an if the most Moslems did not read and understand it? How many scholars I heard reciting the verse of Qor'an improperly so the original meaning might be divergent; and when I asked him he abruptly replied: "I know better than you"; it is bitter but it is a real experience in my life, not one but some.

Chapter One: Brief History of Islam

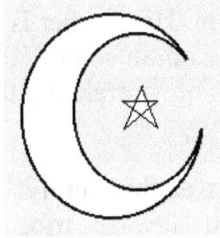

1. Mecca before Islam

This modern world started about 2000 years ago, and the real modern world started when the explosive with a mass destruction capability was intentionally made to destroy the human being. It was a long history of the mankind, but every time the ancient people 'needed to hurt someone else' they used a simple tools like a branch of tree or a stone or even their bare hand, they never used the explosive a most dangerous invention during all time of history. That is our modern civilization today, the modern people even do not know who is the most civilized; we are or they were the primitive people. In the history of mankind, the people always need the divine guidance that is the religion; and all main religions i.e. Judaism, Christianity and Islam started from Abraham. Moses and Isa were sent to Jacob descendants then they split into Judaism and Christianity; Islam came to verify the both with some requirements. Each of all three major religions has its own trace from Abraham the Father of All Believers; their followers have so many reasons to respect each other and no single reason to hurt.

Mecca is located in the central Arab peninsula a point of trade line between Yemen in the southern peninsula and Syria in the Mediterranean. Mecca is well known by the people because there is an ancient building the Ka'bah built by Abraham in about 9000 BC.

In this religious city, Mohammad was born on April 20, 571 AD from the couple of **Abdullah** and **Amenah**. His father is Abdullah son of Abdul-Mutalib son of Hashem son of Abdul-Manaf son of Qusay son of Kelab son of Murrah the descendant of Ismail son of Abraham. His mother is a daughter of Wahb son of Abdul-Manaf son of Zohrah son of Kelab son of Murrah. The both are the descendants of Murrah and the descendants of Ismail son of Abraham.

As a tradition for the wealthy family, he was sent to Halima Sa'diyah a baby sitter of Hawazin tribe outside Mecca; he lived there until five. In the age of six, he accompanied his mom to visit his father's grave yard in Medina; as they came back to Mecca at Abwa' about 23 miles south of Medina his mom passed away, soon he was an orphan. He came back to Mecca with Omm Ayman an Ethiopian baby sitter and then he lived at his grandfather house Abdul-Mutalib, it was not long enough; Abdul-Mutalib the leader of Quraysh tribe was 80 and two years later he passed away. Mohammad has no father no mother and no grandfather at the age of eight, then his uncle Abu Taleb to take care of him.

Mecca and Ka'bah during Mohammad's childhood were decorated with so many idols, the people believed in God but to consider the idols as the means to make them closer to God. There are so many names and forms for the idols, some of them are carved from the stone and some of them made from the food, so if an ancient Arab feels hungry after praying a food idol then he eats it up.

Mohammad was well known as a trustworthy person and was honored the title of **Al-Ameen** -the trustworthy man- when he was hired by a wealthy lady Khadijah, she then married to him. Both Khadijah and Mohammad were the same descendants of Qusay; she was the daughter of Khowayled son of Asad son of Abdul-Ozza son of Qusay. Khadijah was married before to Ateq son of Aabed al-Mahzoomy of the Quraysh tribe; he passed away after having a baby daughter, Hind. A couple years later Khadijah remarried to Nabbasy son of Zurrah al-Taemy of the Quraysh tribe. He passed away after having a baby son, Halal.

2

The title of Al-Ameen is not in vain when there was a sharp dispute between Mecca tribes about who is the most eligible tribe leader to put back the "*Hajar-Aswad*" a black sacred stone as a part of Ka'bah building when it was rebuilt. He came with a wise solution; he took his scarf to put the "Hajar-Aswad" on it and to invite all tribe leaders to bring the scarf together along with "the Hajar-Aswad. The fight between the tribes was evaded!

Mecca is a point of trade line between Yemen in the southern peninsula and Syria in the Mediterranean. It has attracting factors i.e. regular fair at Ukaz where the commodity was exchanged and the contest of poems recitation, it was the time for the visitors to make the sacrifice for the idols at Ka'bah.

As Mohammad grew up as an adult, he realized the deviation in the faith occurred amongst the Mecca people. He tried to contemplate in Hera cave at the Mount of Ray about 3 miles north of Mecca. Here he received the first divine revelation at the age of 40.

2. Islam

At the night of Ramadan 17 to correspond with August 6, 610 AD Gabriel the Angel came and conveyed the divine verse. Gabriel said to Mohammad: "Read", Mohammad replied: "I can not read", and then Gabriel recited: **"Read in the name of your Lord who created. He created the human being from the clot. Read, and your Lord is the Most Generous the Most Honorable. He taught the human being how to write with the pen. He taught the human being everything they do not know" (96:1-5).**

It was a long time about two years and half later when the second revelation came, it was the command from God to spread Islam, **"O Mohammad, wake up and warn the people. Glorify your Lord. Clean up your cloth. Stay away from the idols. And no giving anything in order to get the more. And be patient to carry on your job in the cause of your Lord" (74:2-7).**

Mohammad began to teach his people the ultimate truth, the oneness of the God who has no allies and no relatives. His loyal wife, his uncle's son Ali bin Abu Taleb and his servant Zaed bin Harisah, and his best friend Abu Bakr are the first people who accepted Islam. Abu Bakr then invited his friends Osman bin Affan, Zobeir bin Awwam, Saad bin Abi Waqqas, Abdurrahman bin Aof, Talhah bin Obeidillah, Abu Obeidah bin Jarrah, Arqam bin Abel-Arqam, Fatima bint Khattab, and her husband Said bin Zeid Al-Adawy to embrace Islam. They were the first Moslem generation and called the first embracers, and God granted them the Paradise as the privilege (**56:10-12**).

They used Arqam's house as the center for religious teaching covertly before the revelation of a commanding verse to spread Islam candidly (**15:94**). Mohammad then preached openly to the people of Mecca, and he soon obtained the special attention whether from those who accepted or who rejected Islam.

The Quraysh people began to oppose Mohammad; they considered him to insult their idols and tried to persuade him to stop preaching. They came to Mohammad's uncle Abu Taleb offering the money in lieu of stopping the preach, upon this offer Mohammad replied "O my beloved uncle, if they are offering the sun on my right hand and the moon in my left hand, I will never ever give up". As the Quraysh people knew his strong intention, they imposed the persecution against him and even the physical torture for his followers. In the fifth year of the Prophecy (615 AC), Mohammad suggested his follower to move to Abyssinia (ancient Ethiopia) because he knew there was Najhase a wise Christian King while Mohammad himself stayed in Mecca to carry on Islam with any risk. In this period two prominent Quraysh leaders -who once fiercely opposed Islam- to embraced Islam peacefully; they were Omar bin Khatab and Hamza bin Abdul-Mutalib, Mohammad's uncle.

Meanwhile the Quraysh imposed the harder persecution against Mohammad, nobody of Quraysh tribe allowed to make the business or friendship with the Moslems. This condition prolonged during three years, and in such condition his beloved uncle Abu Taleb passed away, he was 87; and a couple years later his lovely wife Khadijah passed away, too.

4

Both of them are loyal supporters to him, he was so sad to have his two family members passed away while the Quraysh imposed a various sanction against him; he decided to move to the city of Ta'if where the Tsaqef tribe lived, but instead of accepting him the people of Tsaqef threw him the stones, he suffered from severe injury but not-life threatening. The condition was so bad and later the people recalled these years as "Aamol-Hozn", the year of sorrow.

As he returned to Mecca, he preached again on the occasion of public pilgrimage when the pilgrims from city of Yasrib came, they accepted Islam and as they returned to their tribes they spread Islam; soon Yasrib became a conducive for Islam to grow.

The Quraysh after realizing that Yasrib people embraced Islam, they were upset and afraid to lose the influence on the Arab tribes, so they set up a conspiracy to kill Mohammad. He went secretly to Yasrib accompanied by Abu Bakr and Abdullah bin Orayqet as initial guide. Abdullah bin Orayqet went back to Mecca, Mohammad and Abu Bakr were hiding in Tsur cave outside Mecca for a couple days, while the Quraysh were searching to kill them. Later on this dangerous encounter recalled by God in Surah At-Taubah verse 40. **"If you do not help Mohammad then it is no problem because God helped him as the disbelievers (*kafaroo*) drove him out from Mecca when he was amongst two who were inside the cave** (i.e. Mohammad and Abu Bakr). **Meanwhile Mohammad said to his companion: 'Do not worry, because surely God by our side'; then God sent down the tranquility to him and enforced him with the unseen angel army and set down the power of the disbelievers while the power of God is unbeatable. God is the Almighty the Most Wise (9:40).**

On Rabeul-Awal 8, 622 AD, Mohammad and Abu Bakr arrived at Qoba' village about 7 miles from Yasreb, and a couple days later Ali bin Abu Taleb and other companions joined them, they took a rest and built the first mosque. Four days later on Rabeul-Awwal 12 or September 24, 622 AD they entered Yasreb and received the warm welcome, this city then named "Madinatur-Rasool" or The City of Prophet or Medina; that was a milestone in Islamic history. Mohammad's companions who came from Mecca were named the Mohaajeren (immigrants) and the local people who helped Mohaajeren were named the Ansaar (helpers). Mohammad knew that his companions would be home sick; therefore he tied Mohajeren with Ansar in a virtual kinship; he tied Abu Bakr with Harisah bin Zaed, Jafar bin Abu Taleb with Moadz bin Jabal, and Omar bin Khatab with Etbah bin Malek in the Islamic brotherhood. A couple years later this virtual kinship became real as a biological kinship with the legal rights and liabilities. Later on, during the administration of Omar bin Khatab, the milestone of migration to Yasreb was commemorated as the beginning of the Islamic calendar. That was the 1st year of H (Hijrah/the migration), and now is 1433 H.

As they migrated to Medina they ended a period of hardship and oppression in Mecca, they started a new life about 210 miles or 338 kilometers away from their native land. God recalled this incident in Surah Al-Ma'edah verse 30: **"And remember when the disbelievers (*kafaroo*) set a plot against you to imprison you or to kill you or to expel you; they were setting the plot and God is the Best Plotter" (8:30).**

Medina in that time was not a city of Moslems, there were some followers of old divine religion named 'Ahlul-Kitab' or People of The Holy Scripture and some tribes who were still worshiping idols.

They lived together with same language, culture and tradition; Mohammad successfully made a coexistence agreement with non-Moslem residents of Medina. Amongst the clauses in the agreement are:

(1) All worshippers including the Moslems and Jews are free to practice their own religious teachings without any interference.

(2) All worshippers including the Moslems and Jews have the mutual responsibility to defend the city of Yasreb and its residents whenever any invader comes.

(3) The city of Yasreb is sacred it should be respected by any party. The shelter for the law breakers is not available.

Today, this agreement is considered as a revolutionary and smart diplomacy; what Mohammad (4/20/571-6/8/632) did for Yasreb was even better than what Cromwell (1599-1659) did in Ireland.

Mohammad has successfully built "Arkaanul-Islam", the five basic principles of Islam: (1) Shahadah, a confession that God is the one and only Lord, and Mohammad is His Messenger, (2) Five prayers a day, (3) Charity, (4) Fasting and (5) Hajj. He also productively developed the six fundamentals of faith or "Arkaanul- Iman": (1) to believe in one God, (2) to believe in the Angels, (3) to believe in the Holy Scriptures i.e. Abraham manuscripts, Psalm, Torah, Bible or Injeel, (4) to believe in all Messengers, (5) to believe in the Day of Judgment, and (6) to believe in the good and bad fate. The "Arkaanul-Islam" and the "Arkaanul- Iman" are the basic requirements for any Moslem.

Islam was derived from "*aslamtu*" or "I give in my self to God"; it was Abraham declaration when he told his people that he never worshipped the Star, the Moon, or the Sun as they did (**2:128, 6:74-81, 19:47**).

Islam was designed to be a peaceful world religion; therefore it was spreading so fast from Mecca in 610 to Persian gulf, India, Pakistan, China, south east Asia (Malay and Indonesia), Africa and southern part of Europe (Andalusia, Spain) just only in a couple centuries. As a global religion for the mankind, its concept of equality between the people of various races and nations soon gained the warm acceptance around the globe, the mankind in unity and equality is a central doctrine of Islam (**2:143, 2:213**). The diversity of Islam followers then formed a unique civilization in Spain, Africa, India, Pakistan and Southeast Asia.

Islam maintains its acknowledgment toward another divine religions and their followers (see Chapter Five: People of the Holy Scripture), and it grants the security and asylum for another religion followers whenever they ask (see Chapter Six: the Ethics of War). The followers of Mohammad have been appointed as a nation between two nations: Jewish and Christians, **"Thus we have appointed you as a median nation, that you may be witnesses for the mankind." (2:143)**. There is no single verse to command the Moslems to carry on any violence against any party in the world unless for a self defense.

3. The Caliphs

Upon the passing away of the Prophet Mohammad, Abu Bakr was appointed by the majority of the companions as the caliph, he was a close friend and the only one person stayed together with Mohammad in the Hera cave when the Quraysh were searching them to kill. Abu Bakr, the first adult male to embrace Islam ruled for two years with significant developments during his administration. When Abu Bakr passed away, The House of Experts (*Ahlul-Hilli wal-Aqd*) a group of the prominent Mohammad's companions elected Omar as the second caliph, he succeeded Abu Bakr for more than a decade. During his administration Islam spread extensively to almost a quarter of hemisphere in the East and the West, his mission reached Jerusalem, the Persian kingdom, Syria and Africa.

It was a famous incident when his men arrived at Jerusalem, he was preaching before a Friday congregation at Medina mosque when he suddenly said "Go ahead, move!" When he was done with his prayer a companion asked him "What is going on with you, so you said a weird sentence during the sermon?" he replied "I saw my men were in doubt before entering Jerusalem, so I encourage them". When they entered Jerusalem to take control on the Sacred Mosque, some of them were sent back to Medina to report the success to Omar bin Khatab; they told the friends that they heard Omar's voice "Go ahead, move!"

There is another bizarre story when Omar went to Jerusalem; he accompanied by a private guard (some historians mentioned he was Aslam) and a horse. Omar was a supreme commander of Moslem Army, he has a privilege to ride the horse all the trip, but he preferred to share simultaneous riding with his guard; he was a wise populist Caliph. The guard refused but Omar resisted and said "All right, you ride the horse for about seven miles, then I do the same, it would be simultaneous between you and me", his guard agreed. The trip ended and the crowd was welcoming the Caliph when something happened, it was the turn for his guard to ride the horse, and the Caliph was marching on his foot.

Instead of asking his guard to step down from the horseback, he ordered his men to protect Christian people and let them free to practice their religious teaching; he also ordered to maintain the sacred sites in Jerusalem.

Omar was the first Caliph to establish the public treasury and a sophisticated financial audit. He also ascertained the public accountability for the incumbents within his administration. A resident of Egypt filed a complaint to Omar that the governor was in favor of his relative rather than the local residents in a dispute. Omar replied "Go back to Egypt, bring along this bone and give it to your governor"; he made a single straight line with his sword on the bone. As the Egyptian went back and submitted the bone from Omar then the governor was suddenly shivering, he realized that he had to be straight like a straight line on the bone or he will be the bone and flesh (see more about Omar in the Chapter Five: Asbaabun-Nozool).

After twelve years in the administration, Othman bin Affan succeeded Omar bin Khatab as the third Caliph in a democratic election within the House of Experts. Othman ruled for twelve years, during his administration the spreading of Islam continued. He was a democratic Caliph, upon the proposal from the companions to inscribe the Qor'an, he agreed even though such a proposal was declined before.

His consideration was simple because in that time there were so many companions memorized the Qor'an, and now during his administration most of them passed away, so the Moslem needed the definitive text of the Holy Qor'an. He appointed the committee to compile the Qor'an; later on it the compiled Qor'an was named after him the Othmany Qor'an, and it was hand written. He ordered to write down five copies of the Qor'an, sent four of them to the Mosques of Mecca, Kofah, Egypt, and Damascus and kept one in Medina as the definitive text of the Qor'an.

After twelve years in the administration, Ali bin Abu Taleb succeeded him. Ali was Prophet Mohammad's cousin and the first youth to embrace Islam in the early stage of Islamic history. He was well known for his bravery in the battles and also for his eloquent sermons, letters, and wisdom. He was so respectful to Prophet Mohammad and considered him as his supreme mentor; it was Ali whose famous statement "*I am a slave of the man who teaches me even a single letter, if he wills he sells me and if he wills he sets me free*" was quoted for generation after generation.

As he passed away, the rules of the "Al-Kholafaa'ur-Raashedeen" ended; the four caliphs hold the highest respect in the Moslems hearts because they democratically elected by the House of Expert without a single dispute to their legitimacy. The four consecutive Mohammad's successors were named the *Rightly Guided Caliphs* or *Al-Kholafaa'ur-Raashedeen*, since they carried on the leadership for the Moslem community by election and democracy and not by heritage. The democratic election was applied long time ago when the Western World were still in the Dark Age.

4. The Struggle for the Power

During Ali administration there was a fierce dispute from Moawiyya bin Abu Sofyan a governor of Iraq who was appointed by Omar bin Khatab some years before, he declared himself as the Caliph and demanded Ali to resign. Moawiyya was son of Abu Sofyan the leader of disbelievers during Badr War; later on the day of Conquest of Mecca Abu Sofyan converted into Islam. Moawiyya was also the brother-in-law since his sister Ramla married to Prophet Mohammad. Upon Moawiyya's declaration then the House started the legal proceeding, it was advisable for both Moawiyya and Ali to resign, and a reelection would be held soon, they agreed. Ali as a democratic Caliph did not resist the administration with the power nor the violence; he resigned in a hope that the House will establish the democratic reelection. But, as Ali resigned then Moawiyya said: "Ali has resigned, and now I am a legitimate Caliph" without the House approval, Ali was cheated. A caliph was a supreme commander of the army and the head of Islamic administration; it was too precious to fight each other just to hold a temporary administration. Therefore, the House decided that for the interest of Islamic brotherhood, Moawiyya will take over the administration for a while and whenever he resigned or passed away then the next caliph had to be democratically elected, both Moawiyya and Ali agreed once more time; Moawiyya then shifted the capital from Medina to Damascus. But, as Moawiyya held the administration he soon appointed his son Yazed bin Moawiyya as the Prince of Throne, and he established the Omayyad dynasty in 661; surely, the fight between his army and Ali's took place. During Yazed bin Moawiyya administration, the tragedy of Karbala occurred, Yazed's army assassinated the whole family of Ali bin Abu Taleb including his son Hasan bin Ali in an attempt to prevent Ali's descendant from taking over the power in the future.

In this time the first Moslem generation ended, most of Mohammad companions passed away or getting older; and the second Moslem generation was coming. The Moslems in this period were direct descendants of Mohammad companions; Hasan bin Ali and Hosein bin Ali were amongst this second generation. They were named *Taabe'ein* or the following generation, and the third generation was *Tabe'et-Taabe'ein* or the next after the *Taabe'ein*, the later generation the far from living sources of Islam.

The Omayyad dynasty was to last for about a century, and during this time Damascus became the headquarter of political administration which held the political and cultural influences stretched from Central Asia and the border of China in the east to northern Africa, Spain and southern France in the west.

Moawiyya had established a dynasty by any means, so his dynasty ended in pains. The Abbasids took over the administration, and then the capital was shifted to Baghdad. Now, the administration was fully politics unlike the Islamic administration during the Rightly Guided Caliphs (Al-Kholafaa'ur-Raashedeen). Fortunately, Baghdad in that time grew into an outstanding center of education, culture, art, and administration as well.

The Abbasid dynasty ruled for over 500 years but as the time went by, the caliphs lost the actual power, they gradually remained as only the symbolic rulers. So many small kingdoms outside Baghdad reign like the Fatimid, the Ayyubi and the Mamluks who held their own legitimacy and power amongst the people in Egypt, Syria and Palestine.

The Abbasid dynasty was finally toppled and abolished in 1258 when Hulagu Khan the Mongol ruler captured Baghdad; he destroyed the city and ordered his army to throw the valuable books away from the library to Tigris River. Too many incomparable books vanished so the water of Tigris became totally blackened; the historians wept the massacre as a tragedy for the mankind and science.

The most important event during the Abbasid dynasty was the relation between Moslem world and the Western world. The rivalry between them to gain the control of the Holy Site and Jerusalem as the birth of Isa and the station for Mohammad before ascending to heaven to lead Pope Urban II declaring a "war of cross" (the Crusade) in 1095. There were the series of Crusades ever since espoused by various European kings including Richard the Lion Heart. The Moslems finally prevailed in 1187 under the command of Salahudin Al-Ayyubi the Kurd; he regained the control of Jerusalem and defeated the Crusaders (see Chapter Four: Paradigm of Jihad).

For over next two centuries and more the Moslems and the Christians have had their own administration over Jerusalem when the Byzantine kingdom ruled the western world.

5. Spain on the lap of Islam

Aya Sophia *)
you are so beautiful
far away in Spain
you left me alone
long long time ago
so remember me for a while
recall the past glamour
we shared together

*) The part of free translation from a long poem by Egyptian poet Ilya Abu Madhi in the first   decades of 20th century to weep the convert of Aya Sofia mosque into church.

When the Abbasid warriors invaded and captured Damascus, Abdurrahman Ad-Dakhil one of the Umayyad princes escaped the massacre and made the long journey to Andalusia (Spain) to build a new dynasty. That was the beginning of the golden centuries of Islam in Spain. Cordoba a small town was transformed into the glowing capital and the greatest city in Europe in that time.

The Umayyad dynasty ruled Spain for over two centuries until gradually weakened and was replaced by the Andalusia native. The ruler came and went until in twelfth and thirteenth century Andalusia was united with the North African Kingdom by Berber dynasty, but once more time the ruler like the Sharify dynasty of Morocco came and went.

The Moslem power in Spain ended in 1492 when they defeated by joint local Army of Isabella and Ferdinand. The history of Moslem power in Spain since Ad-Dakhil until the last king was so long for almost eight century, they left behind the civilization, descendant and legacy.

Aya Sophia and Alhambra are two among the golden legacy of Moslems in Spain. If there is a big question "why they were defeated and expelled", then the answer is another question: "why they neglected the public service".

6. Ottoman Kingdom

In 1453 Mohamed the Conqueror of Turk conquered "the unbeatable city" of Constantinople and shut the Byzantine kingdom down. From a simple Turk origin he founded the Ottoman kingdom and emerged to dominate over the whole of Anatolia and some parts of European continent. He conquered the east Europe and almost the whole Arab world but Maghreb (Morocco), Mauritania, Yemen, Hadramaut and a small part of the Arab peninsula. Even during the power of Suleiman, the Ottoman army reached Hungary and Austria.

The turning point was September 12, 1683 when the Turks under the command of Kara Mustafa were defeated by the army of Poland King John Sobiesky in the battle of Vienna. Since that time along with the rise of Western and Eastern European powers, the power of the Ottomans began gradually to decline.

Nevertheless, the Ottoman kingdom still stood with the remaining power until the World War I when they defeated by the Western Ally. There was another stage of power when Kemal Ataturk in 1924 controlled Turkey and abolished the Ottoman kingdom which ruled the Islamic world for almost six centuries.

When the Ottoman kingdom ruled the parts of western hemisphere including the Balkans, the Safavid kingdom was established in Persia with Isfahan as the capital in the beginning of fifteenth century, it ruled Persian and a part of India subcontinent for over two centuries. The Safavid collapsed in 1736 when the Afghanis invaded; the next stage was too many short-live kingdoms in Persia like the Pahlavi. The latest king was Reza Pahlavi who exiled when Ayatollah Khomeini to lead the revolutionary movement in 1980's. Reza Pahlavi died and buried in Egypt.

Since the seventeenth century, the shining condition of Moslems around the world slipped into the obscurity and weakness, some other things because the small kingdoms were engaging in the chauvinism and group interest. Even some kings were so busy in collecting the girls in the 'harem' and forgetting the public service. The love of 'dunya' everything related to the present life and hedonism dominated the Moslem leaders since last two centuries until today. The condition of 'ummah' is getting worst; the 'okhowwah' (brotherhood) remains as symbol and does not exist in daily Moslem life. The gap between the royal family and the common people is too wide so there is a royal wedding where the bride and groom to ride a cabriolet golden car while another Moslem can not afford even for a pinch of food, never a full diner.

The general condition of Moslems in the world, however, caught up with poverty, stupidity, uneducated, and bad health; this bad condition even getting severe because some them returned to the ancient tradition: 'asabiya' or chauvinism. Here some of Moslem countries to highlight.

Chapter Two: Moslems Today

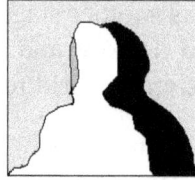

1. Mongol Invasion

When the Moslem rulers were enjoying the *dunya* and neglecting the public service, there was the unknown power came from the East; that was the powerful Mongol from the China Mainland.

The Mongols destroyed the Moslem homelands where Moslem rulers were not aware to what happened beyond their castle. The world knew what happened next; Mongols ruled the lands starting from the northern Arab peninsula to India subcontinent for more than one hundred years (1369 - 1500), later most of them converted into Islam. One amongst their famous rulers was Emir Timur (Tamerlane) who assigned Samarqand as the capital; he successfully blocked the domination of the Ottoman kingdom in the eastern lands.

The Mongol invasion was the second turning point of Moslem history after first one during Omayyad and Abbasid dynasties. Most of the Moslem rulers whether from Omayyad, Abbasid, Ottoman or the others had consider the power as a means of self satisfaction. Yazed bin Moawiyya was an unambiguous example; just for the temporary power he killed the Ali descendant in Karbala massacre, fortunately one baby left behind in the hug of his dead mother, he was Zaenal Abedeen a great grand son of Mohammad the Prophet.

Nevertheless, there was an outstanding King of Omayyad dynasty; he was Omar bin Abdul Aziz who ruled Baghdad in the classic period of Moslem history. When the ruling king passed away, as a Prince he should have been appointed the next King by the House of Representative, a normal process of succession. He was supposed to swear in before the House when he addressed the shocking sermon; he refused to be a King. The reason was simple *"The House had set me up to be a most responsible man before God in the Day of Judgment for the spreading of sins in the land of Baghdad. So ask someone else to be the next King"*, the deliberation was postponed and the Chairman of the House announced a next day assembly.

The assembly was officially open next day when the Chairman found a smart solution. He said to Omar bin Abdul Aziz before the House *"We, the House, appreciated the decision of Prince Omar bin Abdul Aziz. We were going to appoint another King, and if in the future this country would be devastated by the tyrant then we would testify before God in the Day of Judgment that the Prince was a subject to blame, because he gave the tyrant a chance to rule this lovely nation"*. Upon this decisive argument then Omar bin Abdul Aziz accepted the obligation as a King with one condition he said: *"If I ruled along with the Islamic law, then obey me, and if I diverged that's your obligation to fire me"*. His lovely and loyal wife one day wants to show him how smart she is to manage the family expense; she shows him a lot of money she saved from her husband king salary since this family still live so humble as a common people and not as a royal family. Omar bin Abdul Aziz right away called the Secretary of Treasury to take all money his wife saved since he consider his salary was too high; he also order to cut half of his salary off by next month. The time went by, and no a single King compared to him ever since.

2. Afghanistan

The Afghani modern history dated back to 1747 when some tribes formed an administration. Afghanistan is a country with four-season climate, it shares borders with Pakistan in the east and south, Uzbekistan, Tajikistan and Turkmenistan in the north, and Iran in the west.

The majority of the Afghanis are Moslem-Sunni of the Pushtun and other tribes in the east and south, while 10 percents are Moslem-Shia of the Hazaras in the north and west. It is well known that the prominent agriculture in Afghanistan is opium plant, although other crops and the mining are available as well.

The original name of Afghanistan was Khorasan, and during the classic period of Islam there were some scholars whose names ended with Al-Khorasany to indicate their native was Khorasan. In the very beginning of twentieth century when most of Moslem countries occupied and exploited by the western colonialists there was a modern movement for the rise of Moslems in the occupied lands. The leaders of this movement were Mohammad Abduh of Egypt and Jamaluddin Al-Afghani of Afghanistan; they published Al-Manar Journal (1901-1905). Jamaluddin Al-Afghani was one of the most respected scholars in the Moslem world, and he was a founding father of the Islamic Renaissance in Egypt and Afghanistan.

The small difference between Moslem-Sunni and Moslem-Shia in Afghanistan used to be exploited by the outer powers since sixteenth century during the Safavid to generate the fight between them, so the advantages could be obtained after implementing the method of *divide et impera* (scatter and oppress). The difference between two groups of Moslem during 1970's some times escalated to the tribe conflict like the Pushtun as a majority in one side and the Hazaras in the other, or the conflict between Pushtun and Tajiki.

The difference between Sunni and Shia dated back to Omayyad when Yazed bin Moawiyya killed the Ali descendants (see The Chapter One: Struggle for the Power), the Ali followers then established a myth and teaching that named Shism today. The main source of disparity is NOT religious teaching but politics and money.

3. Africa

Islam entered Africa in the era of Prophet Mohammad when his companions migrated to Ethiopia in the fifth year of his Prophecy, 615 AD. The Ethiopian King Najhase accepted Islam but let his people to have their choice.

During the administration of the caliphs, Islam penetrated deeper into the continent and even reached Europe during the Abbasid dynasty (see Chapter One: Spain on the lap of Islam). The Egypt has an unique geographical location which attracted so many powerful rulers since Cleopatra, Mark Anthony, the Ottomans, Napoleon Bonaparte until the British kingdom (see Chapter Three: The Suez Crisis). Egypt is a gate to the continent; the Egyptian Arabs are not the native resident, they came from Arab peninsula since the time of Joseph about 7000 BC far before the 'Bane Esrael' did during Moses era in 5000 BC. Joseph was son of Jacob son of Abraham; later on Jacob named Israel and his descendants named 'Bane Esrael' or sons of Israel. Abraham had two sons Ismail and Jacob; Ismail offspring are Arabs and Jacob offspring are Israel. Therefore Qor'an named them 'Bane Esrael' indicating the close relation with Arabs the other descendants of Abraham.

The famous Egypt ruler Muhammad Ali was not an Egyptian; he was an Albanian who separated from the Ottoman during his administration in 1840's. The modern Egypt started with Gamal Abdul-Nasser Revolution to oust King Farook in 1952, he established the United Arab Republic an Egyptian-Syrian union lasted only for three years, 1958-1961.

During the Nasser administration there was an opposing movement from the "Ikhwaanol-Moslemien" (Moslem Brotherhood) organization, this organization disputed the secular style of the administration. Nasser later executed Muhammad Hasan Al-Banna a prominent author and a member of the "Ikhwaanol-Moslemien", as Nasser passed away then his close friend during 'the Free Army' revolution Anwar El-Sadat succeeded.

Egypt lost Gaza strip and Sinai during June 1967 war with Israel, and six year later Sadat won the Yom Kippur war against Israel in October 1973; he visited Jerusalem in 1977 in search of future peace with Israel. Sadat's popularity spread into the Arab countries even to Israel, his famous personality attracted then-Israeli Prime Minister Golda Meir to say: "He's the first Arab I would like to hug with". The bitterness of war persuaded Sadat to sign the peace treaty with Israel sponsored by the US President James Earl Carter in Camp David. The Accord had generated the 1978 Nobel Prize for Sadat and Menachem Begin (see Chapter Two: Palestine); later on in 2002 James Carter won also the Nobel Peace Prize. Egypt is the first Middle East country to sign the peace treaty with Israel, this to lead to the assassination of Sadat in 1981 during a military parade.

Egypt is a living history; as Vice President Hosni Mubarak was appointed the President, then he ruled for 30 years until The *Tahrir Square* in Cairo occupied by the Egypt people during the Arab Spring. And now, the new President Mohammad Morsi is also facing the classic Egypt problem.

4. India Subcontinent

India, Pakistan and Bangladesh were parts of the Persian and Mongol kingdoms in the past where Islam, Christian, Buddhist and Hindu lived together in the subcontinent. The Moslems initially held the influential political power in the thirteenth century until the beginning of the fifteenth century when Babur a Timur prince conquered India and established the Mogul kingdom. Shah Jahan was one of the famous Mogul rulers built the legendary Taj Mahal -means The Crown of my wife Mumtaz Mahal- the grand mosque, the pool and the mausoleum filled with beautiful marble ornaments. The Kingdom was abolished as British colonialist came to India in 1848.

India declared the independence from British colonialist in 1947, and in the same year it split into India and Pakistan, later Pakistan split into Pakistan and Bangladesh in 1975. The majority of Moslems in India subcontinent to embrace Islam according to Hanafy school; they are pious Moslems and urged to spread Islam peacefully through education and periodical short learning.

The peaceful religious tolerance in India broke apart in 1992 when the Hindu extremists burned out the Babri mosque in the city of Ayodhya, district of Uttar Pradesh. They claimed that the mosque should be torn down and replaced with a Hindu Temple because it was a birthplace of their 'god' King Rama. In fact, King Rama never existed; he was an imaginary king in a legendary Ramayana saga written by Monk Valmiki in the fifth century. The mosque was built in 1527 by order of the Mogul emperor of India named Babur, and was named after him (https://en.wikipedia.org/wiki/Babri_mosque).

The Babri Mosque was destroyed when a political rally broke into a riot involving 150,000 people or more, it was the responsibility of Hindu organizers who broke their promise to the Indian Supreme Court that the mosque would not be harmed. The ensuing riots in many major cities of India such as Mumbai and Delhi killed more than 2,000 people, most of them were Moslems.

The other bloody incident occurred on February 27, 2002 when the local Moslems tried to save a Moslem woman abducted by the armed robber on the train in Godhra, the incident left 58 people died. The Godhra train incident was rumored as a mass killing against the Hindus.

The combination of Ayodhya violence, the Godhra train incident, and the poisonous rumor erupted into the bigger flame. On March 4, 2002 the Hindus searched and killed 489 Moslems in Ahmedabad a city located far enough from Ayodhya. The report said the death toll was 800, and more 30 people were burned out alive in Mehsana district. The humanity watch claimed 5,000 Moslems died, 2,000 Moslem women have been raped and more than 250,000 refugees (www.ImanNet.com). Indian Moslems were terrorized in their country, and nobody defended and protected them. In India, the religious freedom is still low compared those in the US, a most conducive country to practice any religion. It is disputable if the demolition Babri Mosque in 1992 and Ahmedabad massacre lead to the Mumbai attack in November 26, 2008 that killed 166 victims and injured 400 hundred people. Either the Babri Mosque attack with 2,000 Moslem victims and the ensuing killing of 2,400 people in Ahmedabad and Bombay/Mumbai in 1992-1993 or the Mumbai attack of 2008 were the terrors against the humanity, the only difference is the Mumbai attack of 2008 drew the global condemnation while only a very few country condemned the Babri Mosque attack of 1992.

The method of attack, and not the number of victim, most probably which determined the global condemnation; if the terrorists used the bomb or other modern gadgets such as airplane then they are condemned, but when they used the dagger and machete then the world keeps silence because the victim deaths were not heard while death from the explosive was heard aloud!

Meanwhile, in the Pakistani Islamic Republic, the prime ministers and presidents came and went whether democratically elected or self-appointed after *coup d'etat*. India, Pakistan and Bangladesh people may involved in the conflict, but the Moslems in these three countries have agreed on one thing that Sheikh Mohammad Zakariyya Khandlavi author of "***Fadzael-e-A'mal***" (The Excellent Deeds) in the Urdu language was an Indian famous scholar.

The English version of his book was read by most Moslems in India, Pakistan, Bangladesh, Malaysia, USA, Canada and Venezuela.

5. Iraq - Iran

When Iraq and Iran involved in the war, the Iranian spiritual leader Ayatollah Khomeini ordered the Iranian revolutionary guards to hold the US diplomats as the hostages for about two years. The "Operation Blue Light" under the order of US President James Earl Carter failed to evacuate the hostages, the helicopter carrying the commando crashed outside Tehran. This failure brought another failure, Carter was unsuccessful to run for the second presidential term, he was defeated by Ronald Reagan a former Hollywood movie star; the husband of Jane Wyman (ex) and Nancy Reagan.

Saddam invaded Kuwait in the Gulf War (1990-1991) and made the irreparable damages in this tiny but oil-rich country on the Gulf of Persia.

Iraqi President Saddam Hussein was on international highlight for more than two decades (longer than 3 US presidential terms). Iraq and Iran were in a brutal war from 1978-1986. Because Iran ever detained the US diplomats in 1980 then during the conflict, the US supported Saddam Husein with some weapons even the chemicals therefore the US knew well Saddam to have the dangerous weapons. Later in 2002 a former high rank US staff told the reporter why the US supported Iraq. She was quoted to say: "Iraq is lesser of two evils" (NBC TV Nightline, September 17, 2002). In 2003, US invaded Iraq anyway.

6. Nigeria

Since the independence from the British in October 1, 1960 Nigeria is always awash with the blood. Five years later the bloody riot occurred between the ethnic powers, and in 1966 Colonel who later on self-appoint General Yakubu Gowon controlled Nigeria after a bloody *coup d'etat*. Under his administration the Moslems and Christian killed each other, and Biafra separatist movement declared the independence from Nigeria led to a bitter civil war for three years until Biafra surrendered in 1970.

The next bloody coup occurred in 1975 when General Murtadla Refai Mohamed toppled Gowon, the civil administration lived short only under President Shegu Shagari in 1979, and once more time the bloody coup came in 1984 under General Ibrahim Babangida command. Obviously, he realized the existence of the next coup, and before it happens he resigned, now the turn of General Sani Abacha to control Nigeria. In 1993, a presidential candidate Mashood Abiola lawfully won the 1993 election, but instead of being sworn in he was imprisoned and "died from the natural cause" in the prison. Abdul-salam Abo-bakar came after Abacha and General Olosegun Obasanjo came next, he was imprisoned but he was so lucky did not die in the prison and even won the presidential election in 1999.

Sani Abacha was a fortunate leader, when he ruled a country with the Moslems majority; the government was very wealthy from oil export and another mine, so he thought no problem with pocketing the government treasure for himself and his family.

The Abacha saga came to a tragic ending when he allegedly called two entertainer girls from India to Abuja to entertain him, next day on June 8, 1998 the guards found him died. The report said he was poisoned, and the other said he was so exhausted after consuming some spirit-enhancing pills, yet the official announcement stated that he died from the heart attack. At last, Abacha joined Ken Sarowima a Nigerian popular essayist who had been hung upon criticizing Abacha administration. Soon after his tragic death Abacha's wife departed from Abuja airport with the luggage filled with US dollar bills, the airport authority detained her. Now, Abacha needs no more pills.

7. Palestine

There is no enough space or word to depict the pain of the people around Jerusalem since 1948 until now. The Arab/Palestine – Israel conflict was not only to cause the casualties between both Arabs and Israelis but to generate at least four Nobel laureates, too. First, in 1950 it's for Robert Bunche a Harvard professor which became the mediator in the Palestine war during 1948. The second in 1978 for Egypt president Mohammad Anwar El-Sadat and Israeli Prime Minister Menachem Begin, and third in 1994 for Palestinian Leader Yasser Arafat, Israeli Prime Minister Yitzhak Rabin and Israeli Foreign Minister Shimon Perez. The fourth for James Carter in 2002; the Nobel Prizes for those involved the Palestinian peace negotiations indicated how serious the Palestine case is, and unfortunately no signs for the bloodshed to stop.

Arabs and Israelis are the direct descendants of Abraham the Father of All Believers; they should have peacefully lived side by side as a grand family attributed to Abraham with their own ways, too many bloods to shed from his descendants; who will stop now?

8. Saudi Arabia

Saudi Arabia is a country where Ka'bah the point of Moslems' prayer direction located; it is also the native land of Mohammad the last Prophet. Saudi Arabia is a most wealthy Islamic country in the world, and its main income sources are oil export and issuing the visa for the pilgrimage.

The kings of Saudi Arabia are direct male descendant of Ibn Saud the founding father of Saudi Arabia kingdom, and he is traditionally named '*Khadimul-Haramain*' the custodian of two sacred mosques of Mecca and Medina. The king maintains his generosity from generation to generation to distribute the charity to Moslems around the world, and grants so many scholarships to the Moslem students in the Moslem countries. The Arab Saudi Kingdom distributes the annual free millions of Qor'an and its translations in various languages to the Moslem countries.

The contemporary glory of Saudi Arabia Kingdom is splashed with the stigma when so many Indonesian in-house maids (TKW or *Tenaga Kerja Indonesia*) who work within the kingdom jurisdiction came back to their country with the new out-of-marriage babies after the rape and abuse. Saudi Arabia is a nation with strict implementation of Islamic law, why the abusers and rapists never be prosecuted? Do they have the immunity to abuse and to rape? And why the Indonesian government did not protect its migrant workers in Saudi Arabia?

The Indonesian Women Workers in Saudi Arabia are not the slave, but they used to get the treatment like the slave. The abuse to the Indonesian maid who worked for the Saudi household takes place not only in Saudi Arabia, but also in the USA jurisdiction. In December 2001, Princess Buniah al-Saud, a niece of King Fahd was arrested on charges of slapping her Indonesian maid; later Buniah leaved the USA and was sentenced in absentia. Why no such prosecution in Saudi Arabia for the similar case? That is another stigma.

9. Southeast Asia

Siam (Thailand), Malaya, and Indonesia were under the influence of Indian Hindu Kingdom in the fifth century. There were some local Hindu dynasties, the Ramas in Siam, the Srivijayas in Sumatra and the Chandragupta-Mauryas in Java Indonesia mainland.

When the Gujarat merchants traded the commodity in the end of eleventh century to Thailand, Philippines, Malaya and Indonesia they brought along their religion, Islam. The influence of Islam to the local tradition and civilization was strong enough, the Moslems in Pattaya south Thailand developed a unique tradition; they wrote the Malayan language in the Arabic letters better than they did in the Roman.

The first Islamic kingdom in Indonesia was established in the city of Demak Central Java in twelfth century, and soon Islam began to spread throughout Indonesian archipelago with the *"pesantren"* education method established by the nine prominent scholars named *"Wali Songo"*.

Now, Indonesia is the most populous Moslem country in the world; the number of Moslems in Indonesia is more than the total Moslems in Saudi Arabia, Yemen, Egypt, Kuwait, United Arab Emirates, Iraq and Iran. Nevertheless, Indonesia with more than two hundred millions Sunni Moslems is **not** a Moslem state, unlike Pakistan or Saudi Arabia, Indonesia has a secular government which permits almost everything and has no stiff law enforcement.

Chapter Three: Brief History of Violence

War is not only an act of policy, but it is a true political instrument, a (reasonable) continuation of political activity"; Carl von Clausewitz

1. Terrorism

1.1. Violence and Terrorism

The terrorism **is the systematic use of violence as a means of coercion**. Terrorism has a relative meaning depends upon who does say and when. Ireland, Israel and Palestine have a different meaning of terrorism, suicide bombing and the mass murder in the refugee camps of Shabra and Chatila.

Every time there is always a subjective reason for the violence. Every movement group has its radical group and every radical group has its terrorism element. Ireland has IRA, militia group in Oklahoma has Timothy McVeigh who blew up Alfred Murrah Federal Building in 1995 with 186 people died; he was executed in May 2002. Ku Klux Klan in Alabama has Thomas Blanton; he blew up a church in September 15, 1963 leaving 4 African American girls dead.

Back to the history, even a Pope allegedly had the anti-Semitic tendency during the World War II. Eugenio Pacelli (Pope Pius XII) was criticized because his failure to response to the escalating number of the Holocaust where the millions of European Jews killed by Hitler. And there was a dispute over the kidnapping a Jewish boy to be educated and converted into a Roman Catholic priest instead of a Rabbi.

28

The amendment to spare between the state and the religion does not mean that the USA opposes religions; it is a legacy of the Roman *Trias Politica* doctrine and to clear the government institutions (office, courts, schools, etc) from religious practices. The religious practices are considered as the individual freedom, as the freedom to evade the religious practices. The American administration and court system never prosecuted the citizen on the basis of the violation against any religious law.

The terrorism is a continuance of the violence (see the violence cycle below). When two groups have the different idea and implementation on a case –either natural or provoked by third party– then one of them tends to coerce the idea to another. This situation might be inconvenience or even hurts the other party, on this level the alert becomes yellow; it is the third highest alert level. Unfortunately the disappointment is not always expressed clearly until it repeats again just because the other group does not understand what is going on. When the unhappy party needs 'a safety valve' then the light opposition or even the violence occurs to express the annoyance. Now, the alert level becomes pink, it is the fourth highest alert level.

Sometimes this level is intentionally generated to test the combat readiness and to unify the diversified people, for this purpose in 1960's Mao Ze Dong ordered to bombard Que Moy island for a couple weeks constantly because 'the enemy used it as a basis to destroy our revolutionary people'. Que Moy is a tiny island off shore China mainland; it was unoccupied during the bombing.

The violence may attract the terrorism or even the battle, and the battle may escalate to the war. Whenever two groups feel tired in the battlefield they need the third party to intervene. This situation may reduce the alert level and produce a truce, but unfortunately in most cases –like Tanzania Truce between Hutu and Tutsi of Rwanda or Korean cease fire or the Middle East Truce– the involved parties did not comply with, then the violence cycle begins again.

The Arab-Israel, Iran-Iraq, Korean and Asia-Pacific wars were so tight and painful; the western countries knew how painful the war is when they involved in the World War. No single war initiator enjoyed the victory. Hideki Tojo, Benito Mussolini and Adolf Hitler are the examples. Anybody will follow them?

The Violence Cycle and Severity

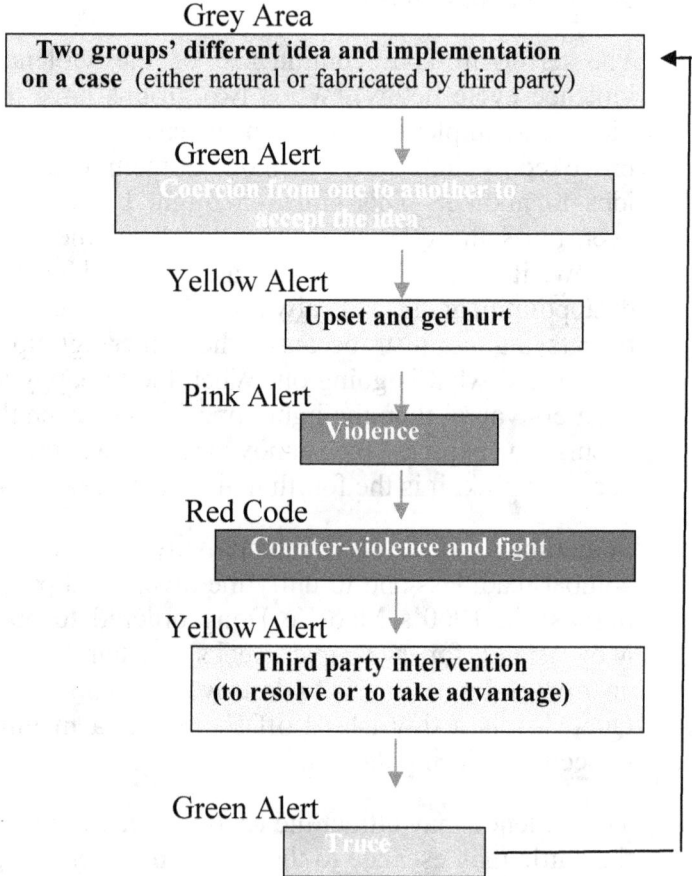

Grey Area

Two groups' different idea and implementation on a case (either natural or fabricated by third party)

Green Alert

Coercion from one to another to accept the idea

Yellow Alert

Upset and get hurt

Pink Alert

Violence

Red Code

Counter-violence and fight

Yellow Alert

Third party intervention (to resolve or to take advantage)

Green Alert

Truce

'The Violence Cycle and Severity' will help us more understanding to the violence and its cycle. The civilized people need no more terrorism and bombing, it will add the long list of casualties and sorrow for so many people. Every group has its own manifestation of coercion, and another group has its opinion whether the coercion is violence or terrorism. The following parts are some selected events to briefly highlight.

1.2. Violence against Moslems

الإسلام محجوب بالمسلمين

"The glory of Islam was covered up by the Muslims themselves."
Mohammad Abduh (1849 – 1905) to reprimand all Moslems
for good; he was a famous *Mujaddid* (Reformer) who lived in
Egypt more than a century ago.

Fourteen centuries ago, by the divine guidance Muhammad the Prophet predicted that the Moslem someday would be like the bubble on the sea going as the wave goes. It depicts that the Moslems would be powerless. Upon narration of this prophecy, his companions asked him "Are we minority?" Mohammad the Prophet answered "No, you are majority but you so deeply love the worldly life (*dunya*) and scare of death."

These two keywords "love the worldly life (*dunya*)" and "scare of death" now are coming. It is not secret that the Moslem leaders are so deeply involved in the worldly life. Bangladesh, Pakistan, and Indonesia with the Moslem majority are full with corruption and deception. Soeharto for 32 year had provided the perfect example how to embezzle the public money with the "smart and legitimate method"; no wonder if the next generation is following him since he never be prosecuted.

With due respect to the Moslems in these countries, statistic has proved that the level of corruption in the countries with Moslem majority such as Somalia, Sudan, Iraq, Afghanistan, Libya, Indonesia, Pakistan and Bangladesh in unbelievable high. With this such condition, it is hard for Islam to expect the full support from the local Moslems; and eventually Islam slips into in individual practice, not even family tradition and not even a community system as practiced during Muhammad the Prophet time in Medina.

At this point, the prophecy of "the Moslems are similar to the bubble on the sea" has come; and the worst thing is the non-Moslems have no any respect to Islam and Moslem since the Moslems themselves do not respect Islam. Here some facts:

(a) Afghanistan became a colony of different foreign countries since the local leaders are competing and killing each other to be the national leader and President, dated back to 1933 and 1973. The statistic proves that Afghanistan ever had more than 10 presidents during 29 years; it ever had 2 presidents in just the same time and had 2 Secretaries of Defense in the same time of another decade, it was also recorded that a Moslem leader established a communist party in order to obtain the power (Chapter Three: 4.1. Afghanistan). Money (Dunya) is the main goal of contemporary Islamic leaders which is quite different with Mohammad Abduh and Jamaluddin Afghani era in 1884.

(b) Iraq was invaded in 2003 for the reason of having the weapon of mass destruction, even though it's proved to be false.

(c) Pakistan the most advanced Moslem country, becomes a killing fields since democratically-elected Nawaz Sharif administration was toppled in 1999 *coup d'etat* by General Pervez Musharaf who so eager to be a President. Pakistan is one and only country in the world which has no sovereignty over its own airspace since it becomes a regular target of foreign drones no matter the reason.

(d) In August 2010, the construction equipment at the site of future mosque in Murfreesboro Tennessee was burned. The local people from various religions gather and sing at Religious Freedom Vigil in Tennessee following mosque construction site fire. This vigil proved that the *religious harmony* in US is quite different with the other countries; it's better or even the best.

(e) In March 2011, Pastor Jones of Florida ordered the burning of Qor'an.

(f) In August 2012 a mosque in Joplin, Missouri was burned to the ground. The solidarity of local Christians who open their local church for Moslems to have the *iftar* dinner of Ramadan proved that the religious harmony in US is quite different with the other countries.

(g) In September 2012, a Toledo mosque was burned. The police later arrested a 52-year-old man, **Randolph Linn** of Indiana. He pleaded guilty to charges of setting fire to the Toledo mosque. Before the judge he said that he was *"riled up" from watching Fox News TV and consuming beers.* When was asked if he knew any Muslims, he replied, *"No, I only hear on Fox news and what I hear on radio..... Muslims are killing Americans and trying to blow stuff up.......Most Muslims are terrorists and do not believe in Jesus Christ."* Likely, he does not know that believing Jesus as one among 25 Messengers is the fourth pillar among six pillars of Islamic faith. To prevent the similar incident in the future, the Moslems have the obligation to spread the truth that Moslems believe in Jesus who his real name in Aramic was Isa, Peace Be On Him.

(h) In September 1994, the almost completed mosque in Yuba City California was burned down, and nobody ever arrested. On April 26, 1995 the fire destroyed a mosque in High Point, North Carolina. On July 1995, the vandals severely damaged a mosque in Huntsville, Alabama.

The American-Arab Discrimination Committee, a Washington-based civil rights organization reported that in

1991, 119 incidents happened to the American Moslems from spitting to burning the mosques. The New York Times reported that during 1994, five American mosques have been burned down or seriously vandalized. In 1995, 222 attacks against Muslims were recorded. It happened even before 9/11/2001, so what's the matter?

2. Africa

2.1. Angola: time changed

When Angola under Portugal colonialism, there were two major independence movements MPLA a Soviet and Cuba supported group and UNITA a US and South Africa supported group, they were competing to gain the political influence and power.

As Portugal left Angola in 1975, the rivalry between two groups was increasing; in 1994 the United Nations sponsored the truce signed in Lusaka, Zambia; but it collapsed in 1998 and the civil war was unavoidable. MPLA prevailed, and UNITA under Jonas Savimbi was continuing the guerilla for almost 27 years until February 22, 2002 when President Jose Eduardo dos Santos army of the prevailing MPLA involved in the gunfight with UNITA and shot Savimbi to death.

MPLA and UNITA traded accusation, MPLA claimed that UNITA is the terrorist because it blocked the international aid for the poor during the famine, and UNITA claimed that MPLA was the terrorist because it did not comply with the UN sponsored truce.

If this happened during the Cold War, Santos would have received the condemnations from around the world, but now who does care?

2.2. Algiers: the winner of election cancelled

The modern governments around the world were established on the basis of democracy, but when Abdel Aziz Bouteflika's administration supported by armed forces to cancel the democratic victory of the Front of Islamic Salvation (FIS) in 1992, is any government in the world to criticize Algeria?

The cancellation has suspended due process for the democratization and to rise up the fighting between the government security forces and the disappointed groups. The government said the operation was a counterterrorism action, but FIS said the security forces violated the human rights and committed the serious abuse to the democracy. On November 22, 1999 Abdelkader Hachani a prominent FIS leader who had preached for peace and reconciliation, was shot to death in the capital, nobody knew who did.

Who is the subject to blame when the rally and even the uprising occurs. The domino effect of the continuous fight was unavoidable. FIS and Bouteflika traded accusation on who is the terrorist, and the outcome is 300,000 people died. So, who is the real terrorist? Why it's too easy to kill 300,000 lives?

2.3. Central African Republic: 'Emperor' Bokassa

Central African Republic is a tiny secluded land not larger than Ohio, but it had a notorious 'Emperor' Bokassa. As a colonel in the Army he had several subordinate soldiers under his command, so in 1971 he took over the power and proclaimed himself the president. Because he was a supreme leader he needed more girls, nobody knew how much, but the people knew his children, more than 60.

He maintained the good relation with France and sent some carats of diamond to France President Valery Giscard d'Estaing, unfortunately this relation was slip-tongued as "Giscarat", and on the next term d'Estaing was unsuccessful to run the presidency.

When the presidency was not enough for Bokassa, he crowned himself an emperor and ordered to oppress the 'extremist'. He allegedly ate the flesh of his enemy, and he was named a 'Cannibal Emperor'. There were some gold and diamond mines in Central African Republic, so what's wrong if his imperial chair depicted the huge golden peacock - definitely it was the real gold- and his crown was scattered with the diamonds. The world is never enough; too many violence during his regime and nobody stopped him, even his insanity was considered as an amazing opera.

2.4. Egypt (1): The Suez Crisis

Everyone knows The Suez Canal is in Egypt soil, but when the Egyptian president Gamal Abdel Nasser took control on the Suez Canal on July 26, 1956, the war erupted. Nasser and Arab League demanded the Moslem countries to pledge the support and to make a special prayer called "*Qunut Nazelah*". They prevailed, and Suez remained on the hand of Egypt; unfortunately most Moslems today do not know how to say the "*Qunut Nazelah*" prayer.

The England and France were considering that Suez nationalization was a threat to the oil shipment from Persian Gulf to Europe. They were allying with Israel and confidentially preparing a military operation to regain the control of the Suez Canal and, to topple Nasser.

On October 29, 1956, Israeli troops invaded Egypt. The England and France were playing the good scenario to demand "each party should withdraw from the canal zone and to cease fire immediately". When Soviet Union was threatening an intervention, the war ended on December 22, 1956.

2.5. Rwanda and Burundi: the tragic presidents death

Hutu and Tutsi are two competing tribes to gain the political influence and the power over Rwanda, after a long rivalry they signed an agreement in Tanzania on August 1993. The peace agreement collapsed when the Hutu considered the Tutsi as discriminative in the administration while the Tutsi considered the Hutu preferring the violence.

April 6, 1994 was a very tragic day for two nations, Rwanda and Burundi; they lost their presidents in a mysterious plane accident, a terrorist attack? A plane with two presidents on board exploded. Habyarimana, president of Rwanda and Cyprien Ntaryama, president of Burundi died in the accident; it was assumed that the plane carrying them shot down by the Hutu even nobody had proved or refuted, Habyarimana and Ntaryama were Tutsi.

The wave of chaos and mass killings occurred for the next months after the death of two presidents, almost 1,000,000 civilians of Tutsi and Hutu of Rwanda were killed. Hundreds of thousands of them fled into eastern Zaire where their relative of same tribe lived, they returned to Rwanda three years later.

The latest atrocity is the killing of 173 civilians of Burundi on September 9, 2002 to increase the death toll up to 500,000 since the rivalry between Tutsi and Hutu of Burundi getting worst after the death of Ntaryama. The Burundi Tutsi government and Hutu traded accusation.

The tragic presidential deaths in Rwanda and Burundi are incomparable sorrow in the history of world administration, and the mass murder following the incident was the worst tragedy in the competing tribal history.

2.6. Uganda: Idi Amin Dada

Africa is a black continent but its mining is bright and shining, therefore some 'civilized nations' took it as the colony and piggy bank. Uganda is one of the suffering nations from the inhumane colonization. If the descendants of holocaust in Israel successfully filed the lawsuit against the parties involved in the atrocity, then the ex-colony countries should have done the same legal action or class action against the ex-colonialists.

In Uganda, it is not necessary to ask what the education is; the educative and administrative job is beyond the thought of most people. When a giant youth with 240 pounds weight and 170 cm height cannot afford a good education and administrative job then a career as a professional boxer is not a bad choice. That was Idi Amin Dada (Dada means The Father); he was a Ugandan national boxing champion for more than 8 years! The strong body is the good asset to join the Army, so that he did; it was amazing that as an elementary school dropout he reached a high rank in the Army under General Milton Obote, the Ugandan first president.

When Obote went abroad for an official duty in 1971, Idi Amin thought that the President left behind the country and it was not good for a nation without a president, so he took the administration over in a successful *coup d'etat*.

He enjoyed the power and kept everything under his control, he ordered the killing, rape and even the invasion to the neighboring countries. The uprising? He ordered the mass detention for the 'terrorists', some prisoners were found dead with incomplete body, and some of them were forced to commit a "dog fight" with the hammer to death.

He survived more than 20 assassination attempts, and if the neighboring countries criticized then he challenged their presidents to fight in the boxing arena, Julius Nyerere of Tanzania and Yomo Kenyata of Kenya never answered this crazy challenge. Later, Tanzania invaded Uganda only after Idi Amin's Army occupied Tanzanian border.

The final result was millions of dollars debt, famine, disease, refugee and the irreparable psychological damages for the innocent people. He was a terrorist, but who did prosecute him?

3. America and Caribbean

3.1. Chile: Augusto Pinochet

Salvador Allende democratically won the presidency in September 1970, and in 1973 the Armed Forces of Chile put the presidential palace under siege. The official reason was 'the Armed Forces and the nation of Chile had lost the respect to Allende administration'. Allende was legally elected, he won the election after joining hand in hand with a various political groups including the communist party even though he was not a communist; he was a simple physician who had chosen his way of life.

The official announcement about Allende was 'to shot himself', nobody can confirm nor refute; but the fact was Allende died on *September 11, 1973*. Why this date used to be bloody?

The purge started when the new administration was under the control of the Junta and Augusto Pinochet was the President. During seventeen years of tenure, Pinochet with his 'Caravan of Death' kidnapped, killed, and terrorized his opponents until 1990. There was the official announcement of Allende death but not for death toll, the analysis estimated around 1,000. Pinochet has proved himself as a strong man even after his presidency. He was 'detained' more than one year in Britain when he underwent the medical checkup but was released without indictment although a British citizen disappeared in Santiago during Pinochet administration. Even in January 2001, the Chilean Supreme Court ruled Pinochet should not been brought to justice because of his 'health problem', a good jurisprudence for the next dictator, Soeharto seemed to emulate Pinochet trick.

3.2. Cuba: Fidel Castro

Fidel Castro ruled Cuba after toppling General Fulgencio Batista, Castro is not a general but he prefers to wear the military uniform as Sadam Husein did. Castro was a terrorist against the US when he intentionally allowed the Soviet Union to install the long-range nuclear missile in the culmination of Cold War era in October 1962; no one did it to the US ever since. Castro is a happy and popular terrorist who enjoyed the wide publication on the US TV stations especially after Elian Gonzales case, the interview with Barbara Walters and the coverage on the commemoration of 40 years of the Cuban crisis.

The Bay of Pig incident an attempt to invade Cuba has prompted Nikita Khrushchev then-the Soviet Union Prime Minister to address at the UN Assembly, he pulled out one of his shoes and knocked it to the UN podium, and no one did it before!

He came to power after -who won the internal struggle of power after jailing **Lavrentiy Beria** a hard rival and Interior Minister. His son Sergei is calmer; he prefers to immigrate to US and to be a peaceful citizen; but later he hardly criticized the Bush administration during a speech in Cleveland, October 2002.

Castro (1926-) is 87 and is still going strong; it is not surprising because he was the school best athlete in 1944. Soeharto, the Indonesian leader of New Order, wanted to challenge Castro in the length of presidency but was forced to resign in 1998.

Castro is the president since Kennedy era; some US Presidents came and went since John F. Kennedy, Lyndon B Johnson, Richard Milhous Nixon, Gerald Ford, James Earl Carter, Ronald Reagan, George Bush Sr., and William Clinton while Cuba still maintains Castro. He is still a champion in the length of presidency.

In October 2002, the living actors in Cuban crisis such as Castro and Robert McNamara a former Secretary of State during Kennedy administration reunited in a seminar to commemorate 40 years of Cuban crisis where US was on the brink of a nuclear war. All of them retired from the government but Castro; Khrushchev and Kennedy were not invited, they passed away.

3.3. Haiti: Papa Doc

He was a physician and an educated politician amongst the common people, when he was elected the Haitian President the people called him Papa Doc (Mister Doctor) Duvalier. Papa Doc ruled Haiti from 1957 to 1971 as a politician and dictator unlike a doctor who is taking care of a patient, and he was called 'doctator'.

There was the uprising to replace him but ended with the oppression. Upon his retirement he appointed his son the President of Haiti. As a new president the son ruled Haiti the way his father did, therefore the simple Haitian people called him Baby Doc Duvalier, the son of Papa Doc. The Haiti economics and social arrangement were so bad but not for the Duvaliers, they were the first Haitians to possess a private airplane.

The bad condition is still shadowing Haiti when Jean Bertrand Aristide is ruling Haiti, but the good news is an attempt of *coup d'etat* was thwarted on December 17, 2001 even though Haiti remains one of the unfortunate countries in the world.

3.4. Timothy McVeigh

Timothy McVeigh a US Army veteran was young, energetic and brave; but he used his bravery to terrorize the people by bombing a Federal Building in Oklahoma City on April 19, 1995 leaving 168 people dead including 19 children. Soon after the incident a warden at the Federal Prison was reported to say "I'll bring him to the gurney" without even knowing who destroyed Alfred Murrah Federal Building and before McVeigh indicted.

When he was convicted and sentenced to death he gave up the appeal, his action drew the public attention and a question. This terrorist was executed on June 11, 2001 with a lethal injection. The warden wish was fulfilled.

3.5. September 11, 2001

The terror on US soil on September 11, 2001 was a tragedy where more than 2,800 people dead. Whosoever behind the 9/11 tragedy and benefited from this horrible disaster and whatever the motives of this painful catastrophe; it was a big loss for Moslems and America. Nobody thought that the momentum of 9/11 could be used to justify so many things never imagined before.

The 9/11 was so well known so many TV stations and newspapers reported the tragedy; the further explanation is not necessary. The War on Terror costs two billion US dollars per month; it is a huge amount; it is sufficient to feed the starvation in Africa for a year. More than $15 billions has been spent since the operations began, this amount is not included the cost to clean up the debris at World Trade Center. We need no more violence; so how come Rev. Jerry Falwell (1933 – 2007) determined that we are the Americans suffered from the September 11, 2001 attacks because of our loose morals, is our pain not enough?

3.6. Boston Marathon Bombing

The marathon sport event is not fun anymore since April 15, 2013 when 2 "pressure cooker bombs" exploded in crowd of spectators near the Boston marathon finish line. The first bomb went off a couple seconds before the second in two separated places injuring 264 people and killing 3 spectators at the scene. After a careful investigation, on April 18, 2013 the authority released the photographs of two suspects; they were identified as Dzhokhar Tsarnaev and Tamerlan Tsarnaev.

The situation got worse when one police officer died from shooting on April 18, 2013; one suspect Tamerlan Tsarnaev died and 16 police officers were injured during gun fighting on April 19, 2013. Dzhokhar Tsarnaev was injured but escaped before captured when was hiding in the boat; he was on the pool of blood.

To prevent such an incident from happening again in the future, the US Department of Justice should have cooperated with the Imams across the US. The Moslems are still scarier from being excommunicated by the Imam rather than the police.

Tsarnaev Brothers were not known as the mosque activists; nor did they attend the regular prayer in the local mosque; there must be an actor behind their actions beyond Imam – Congregation traditional relationship. They must be indoctrinated for a long time; they are too young to understand the poisonous brainwashing; Tamerlan was 26 and Dzhokhar is 19. Without proper understanding of jihad, it would have easily slipped into bloody terror. Now, it's the time to bring the preacher of violence to justice.

3.7. Peru: Tupac Amaru

Alberto Fujimori was born and raised in Peru from the Japanese descendant, he was eligible to be elected the Peruvian President, but when his main aide Montesinos deposited more than forty million US dollar the uprising erupted.

The Indian Peruvians were complaining Fujimori about the economics and job opportunity, and when the situation was not getting better then Edgar Sanchez lead the Movimiento Revolucionario Tupac Amaru (MRTA) commando to occupy the residence of Japan Ambassador from December 1996 to April 1997. The residence of Japan Ambassador was chosen just because Fujimori ancestor came from Japan. This movement used a legendary name of Tupac Amaru an Indian leader killed by Francisco de Toledo the Spanish colonialist in 1572.

Montesinos was the Chief of Peruvian Intelligence when the incident happened; he ordered the Peruvian counter terrorism troops to perform the regular exercise in the field next to the residence of Japan Ambassador. To maintain the high spirit of the troops, Montesinos ordered the technicians to install the amplifier to air the mars songs. The real purpose of airing the mars songs was to conceal the noise came from the digging machine to make the artificial tunnel.

On April 22, 1997 the counter terrorism troops emerged from tunnels just in front the residence of Japan Ambassador and killed all MRTA commandos including a MRTA teenager begging his safety.

4. Asia

4.1. Afghanistan

The history of Afghanistan is a tale of cheating, blood and tears. For more than 50 years Afghanistan has been in recurring coup, president assassination and war. No single country in this civilized world lost so many presidents in the bloody coup equal or more than Afghanistan did, a very sad condition to ignite the refugee exodus, famine and foreign intervention.

The contemporary history started from King Nader Shah assassination in 1933, and his son King Mohammad Zahir Shah was toppled by ex-Prime Minister Mohammad Dawood in 1973 in a *coup d'etat* after ruling Afghanistan for 40 years.

The chaos has been ignited, and its flame has extended to Karmal, Taraki, Amin, Najibullah, Mujaddedi, Rabbani, Omar, and Karzai. Each time these men stepped to the stage of presidency each time the blood was shed and next coup was shadowing. Here is a simple statistics, time: 29 years, president(s): 10 more, average term of presidency: less than 3 years, the shortest presidential term: 3 months, killed: hundreds of thousand civilians; result: nothing but casualties. The following incidents may disclose what happened:

1965:   PDPA
          People's Democratic Party of Afghanistan
          (PDPA) a pro Moscow Afghan communist party
          founded by Babrak Karmal and Muhammad
          Taraki.

1973:   Dawood
          King Mohammad Zahir Shah toppled by ex-Prime
          Minister Mohammad Dawood in a *coup d'etat*, he
          supported by the communists.

1978:   Amin and Taraki
          (1) Dawood killed by Hafidzullah Amin troops.

          (2) Nur Mohammad Taraki a new President, and
          Amin the Prime Minister

          (3) Taraki purged Babrak Karmal old friend in
          PDPA, the latter exiled.

1979:   Amin, Karmal, and *Mujahedeen*
          (1) Amin killed Taraki; Amin became a new
          President for less than 2 years including his term
          as Prime Minister, 1978-1979; his term as a
          President lasted for three months only. In
          February 1979, US Ambassador Adolph Dubs
          assassinated by an unidentified killer.

          (2) Soviet President Leonid Brezhnev sent 70,000
          troops to Afghan after Taraki assassination,
          Afghan – Soviet war began and lasted for 10
          years.

          (3) Babrak Karmal came back from exile; he
          killed Amin under Soviet's support.

(4) The *Mujahedeen* established to fight Soviet. In this year, *Mujahedeen* (the Warriors) under the command of Ahmad Shah Massoud were fighting Russian troops and communists in Afghanistan. The US, Saudi Arabia and Pakistan provided Massoud and Osama the materials, money and sophisticated weapons as well.

5) Saudi Arabia, Pakistan and the USA joined hands in hands to support the *Mujahedeen* with money, training and sophisticated weapons. Later, the weapons were bought back by the US in 2002 during campaign against the Taliban.

1986:   Najibullah
Ahmad Zai Najibullah replaced Karmal under the Soviet pressure.

1989:   *Mujahedeen* in Pakistan, 2 presidents
(1) The Mujahedeen in Pakistan established Afghani Government in exile with Sibghatullah Mujadeddi as president; meanwhile Najibullah stills a President in Kabul. Afghanistan is the one and only country to have 2 Presidents in the same time.

(2) The city of Jalalabad was under siege by the *Mujahedeen*, 10,000 people killed.

1992:   Mujadedi, Rabbani, Omar
(1) Massoud's *Mujahedeen* entered Kabul and ousted Najibullah.

(2) Sibghatullah Mujaddedi ruled for six month only. Burhanuddin Rabbani became the President while Hekmatyar opposed him. Rabbani ruled for less than two years only before ousted by Omar.

1993:   Hekmatyar, Dostum
(1) January: Rabbani to fight Gulbuddin Hekmatyar, thousands of civilians killed.

(2) March: Hekmatyar was appointed as prime minister, after refusing in 1992. The fighting erupted because the unsettled status of two Defense Ministers Massoud from *Jamiat-e-Islami* party and Abdu-Rashed Dostum from the *Communist Party*. General Dostum was a War Lord whose troops allegedly raped and killed Afghani women. Afghanistan is the one and only country to have 2 Secretaries of Defense in the same time.

(3) June: Hekmatyar was sworn in as Prime Minister; Massoud resigned.

1994:   *Taliban*
Mohammad Omar established the *Taliban*; he gave the shelter to Osama, now his existence is unknown after US bombing. Osama in 2011 was killed in Pakistan by US Navy Seals.

1996:   *Taliban* vs. *Mujahedeen* and *Northern Alliance*
(1) Taliban invaded Kabul in September, and hanged Najibullah to death.

(2) The *Mujahedeen* was reuniting again with other factions. Massoud, Dastoum, Rabbani and other Afghani leaders formed "*Northern Alliance*" to fight against Omar's Taliban.

2001:   End of Massoud and Taliban
(1) Just one day before 9/11, Ahmad Shah Massoud the *"Lion of Panjshir"* who defeated Brezhnev and forced Gorbachev to pull the Russian troops out of Afghanistan assassinated by the unidentified killer. Is it any correlation?

(2) September 11 terror attacks on World Trade Center, New York; leaving about 2,900 dead. US and the Northern Alliance pressed Taliban to hand Osama bin Laden over.

(3) The US to bomb Taliban. Abdul-Hamid Karzai elected President.

(4) Haji Abdul Qadir the Vice President, was killed in August 2002, his brother executed by Taliban in 2001.

2002:   Karzai
          Abdul-Hamid Karzai saved from two attempted murders in July 2002 and September 2002.

The power and administration came and went year after year, decade after decade, nothing eternal, everything is changing, the never-changing thing is the changing itself, that is God's doctrine **"And there are the days We grant them to the people by turns" (3:140)**. Afghanistan is a rich country with natural resources; whosoever rules Afghanistan he will hold a real power. It is no surprise if some people want to hold Afghanistan by any means, although for a while; but if any candidate of Afghani President read the statistics and realized how many presidents and vice presidents killed during last 29 years he should have canceled his candidacy.

Since more than 50 years ago, no single succession in Afghanistan came **without** violence or bloodshed, how amazing this fact is. Gulbuddin Hekmatyar (2002) former Afghani Prime Minister the leader of *Hezb-e-Islami* is shadowing Karzai administration. Is he a future Afghani President?

During 29 years, Afghanistan has 10 presidents, average term of presidency less than 3 years, the shortest presidential term 3 months; number of killed: hundreds of thousand civilians; other result: nothing but casualties. If a president rules more than 3 years then he would survive more 3 years but with some attempted murders.

4.2. Cambodia

His name became identical with the killing field of millions people when he was the Prime Minister of Cambodian Communist government, and he lived so lonely in his last years in the jungle; he was Saloth Sar.

The world knows him as Pol Pot (1925-1998) a cold-blooded killer who led the Red Khmer guerrilla troops to overthrow the pro-Hanoi government and Lon Nol regime in 1975. Lon Nol was a Cambodian president after toppling the King Norodom Sihanouk (1922 – 2012).

Pol Pot ordered the killings about two million Cambodians, the report said that the execution used to be deliberated by the young Red Khmer guerillas, some of them are teens. The young guerilla then decided whether the group of detainees should be executed or sent to prison for torture and hard labor.

The bad day came to him on 1979 when Vietnam invaded Cambodia to oust him after a border dispute. Pol Pot went back to the jungle, and when the new government was going to prosecute him for his "killing field", he fled to Thailand border. The former Prime Minster and former Buddhist monk who terrorized the Cambodian people for almost a decade killed himself in April 1998. Any attempt to bring him to justice has been blocked by the Chinese government.

The communist history is always full with the terror and mass killing, and now after Pol Pot died nobody to take responsibility for the Cambodian massacre. Most of us do not agree with the Pol Pot style to kill his people, but China did. China vetoed the international tribunal on Pol Pot; that is the fact.

4.3. China

The history of communist party is always stained with so many bloods. The Chinese Communist Party (CCP) during and after Mao Ze Dong (1893-1976) era was not an exception. Mao might be the most powerful state leader who ever lived after Pharaoh, and his dress code – the cotton jacket with a rounded collar style- followed by more than one billion people for more than 25 years to make the international dress designers and fashion stars jealous of him. He enjoyed the popularity and the obedience of his people more than six US presidential terms consecutively.

The rivalry between Mao Ze Dong and Chiang Kai Shek (1887 – 1975) was a rivalry between Kun Chang Tang (communist) and Kuo Min Tang (nationalist) over the people in the China mainland which is wider than the USA with so many natural resources.

Mao adapted so many ancient wisdoms from Kong Hu Tzu (Confucius) to win the rivalry, here the some:

(1) "If you are going to deter the lion in the jungle you need to kill a monkey".

(2) "If you have to send your friend to prison, say with a good manner: 'You are sick my friend, you need a medicine'"

(3) "If you have the strong enemy, consider the enemy of your enemy as a temporary friend". It happened in 1937 when Chiang Kai-Shek was arrested by the disappointed Kuo Min Tang youths. Mao stunned the friends and foes when he sent Chou En Lai to beg for Chiang's life to join hand to fight Japan. But as Japan went, Mao smashed Chiang in a bloody civil war (1946-1949).

(4) "If you do a purge, say to your supporters: 'We should distinguish between fragrant flowers and poisonous weeds'". Upon this notorious wisdom, Chiang Kai-Shek in 1927 ordered the Shanghai massacre, a mass killing of tens thousands of communist members. Mao did the same when he ordered to 'pull out the poisonous weeds'; the result was 3,000,000 people killed from 1950 to 1975.

Mao joined Kuo Min Tang in 1925 when he was weak and when got the enough power he kicked Chiang Kai Sek out to Formosa Island; therefore he eliminated his close friends Lin Piao (1907 – 1971) and Liu Sao Chi (1898 – 1969) first before they did the same. And, Deng Xiao Ping did what Mao did during Tian An Men uprising, and Jiang Ze Min then-President of People's Republic of China from 1993 to 2003 was doing against the Falun Gong movement. Jiang Ze Min is the third generation of China Communist leader who still understood and applied the *oriental wisdom* of Confucianism; with this kind of wisdom he made both China Communist Party and China Military Commission his supporters to the presidency while both his successors failed. This *oriental wisdom* is a 'smart' choice the West failed to understand, this is a Chinese style of "Pek Maa Tui Hong". Jiang's two successors Hu Jintao (China President from 2003 to 2013) and Xi Jinping (China President from March 2013 to now) were only supported fully by the China Communist Party and not China Military Commission. Jiang is a true Chinese leader behind China prosperity today. Mao, the main Chinese leader fulfilled an ancient wisdom *"Who has the long life and holds the power, he has a real happiness"*, he did what no Afghani President did.

4.4. Indonesia: The Killing General

1945. Soekarno and Mohammad Hatta on the behalf of Indonesian people declared the independence on August 17. Three months later, the City of Surabaya East Java mainland occupied by the Allied Forces under the command of British General Malaby on November 10, 1945. Malaby was pretending to take Japanese forces into custody, but he concealed Dutch Army in an attempt to takeover Indonesia again and to take benefit from the critical time. When the Surabaya people saw the reality, they fought the British and Dutch troops.

Malaby distributed the fliers from the plane to intimidate people to surrender, but Bung Tomo a Surabaya leader addressed a radio speech to encourage people to fight and never give up. Twenty-two years later in 1977, the England was so eager to know if Indonesian was going to revenge over the cheating of British General Malaby during the Surabaya battle, and for this purpose the England sent a female spy under the disguise of "leading British reporter" to interview the Indonesian Vice President Hamengku Buwono IX, since he was the living actor of historical events during Indonesian struggle for freedom.

1957. The separatist movement in Sulawesi Island announced the establishment of "Permesta" (Perjuangan Semesta Alam or Charter of Common Struggle Movement) on March 12, 1957.

1957. On December 7, 19:39 local time at Subic Bay, The Philippines; Admiral Felix Stump the commander of US Pacific Fleet received a very urgent message from Admiral Arleigh Burke to move from Subic Bay to Sulawesi Island East Indonesia. They were so in a hurry and never thought for what reason the fleet entered the Indonesian territory. Later they found a good reason, Stump called Colonel Ahmad Husein a PRRI/Permesta rebel to invade Caltex a US oil company based in Pakanbaru, Sumatra. If a US company were under attack it would be a good reason for US Fleet to go to Indonesia. Husein had no time to do because General Abdul Haris Nasution sent the troops to subdue the terrorists.

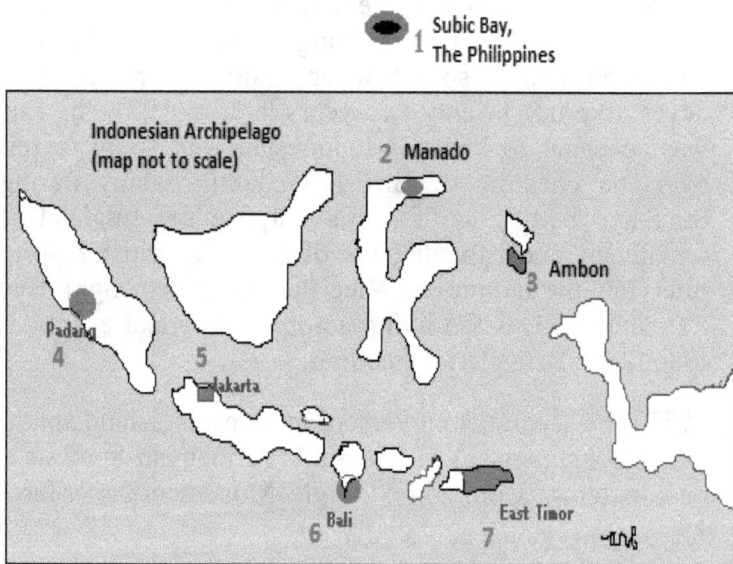

1 Subic Bay, The Philippines

Indonesian Archipelago (map not to scale)

2 Manado

Ambon
3

Padang
4

5 Jakarta

6 Bali

7 East Timor

1. Subic Bay, The Philippines; command control of Permesta rebels
2. Manado, Permesta rebel headquarters
3. Ambon Island, site of mercenary pilot Allan Pope was shot down
4. Padang, West Sumatra; PRRI rebel headquarters
5. Jakarta, Indonesian capital
6. Bali, site of October 12, 2002 bombing
7. Timor Leste

1958. The people of West Sumatra Island announced an administration separated from Soekarno, they established "Pemerintah Revolusioner Republik Indonesia" (The Revolutionary Government of Republic of Indonesia/PRRI). Later PRRI and Permesta joined hand in hand and named PRRI/Permesta. Soekarno assigned General Abdul Haris Nasution to subdue the rebellion. The PRRI urged Indonesian President Soekarno to dismiss the Presidential Cabinet under the 'secular' Prime Minister Mohammad Djuanda and to replace with 'the revolutionary people'.

Instead of complying with the demand, Soekarno and Army Commander General Abdul Haris Nasution sent the troops and bomber planes to Padang the capital of West Sumatra province. PRRI was totally eliminated in March 1958.

February 12, 1958 Padang was bombed and a native Padang scholar then-Rector of University of Indonesia Prof. Bahder Djohan resigned, he was one and only rector of state university to resign. He's the man.

1958. May 18, a B-26 bomber with pilot Lieutenant USAF Allan Lawrence Pope and copilot Corporal IAF/AURI Harry Rantung on board were shot down in Ambon Island. They were hired by PRRI/Permesta to drop the explosives to Indonesian Fleet heading to Manado, North Sulawesi to subdue the rebellion.

Soon after the incident, US Attorney General Robert Kennedy left for Jakarta to bring US President Dwight Eisenhower's private letter to Soekarno asking him to set AL Pope free, Soekarno granted the freedom for Pope. To reduce the tension, the next US President John Fitzgerald Kennedy invited Soekarno to Washington, Soekarno initially declined after considering his own safety and, he realized that Pope was involved in a rebellion to topple his administration. Kennedy assured Soekarno's safety before visiting Washington. Two years later, he was very sad to hear the assassination of Kennedy in Texas.

1965. September, the most villagers in Indonesia woke up very early before 03:00 AM in the morning to watch the east sky to see the comet with a very long tail. It was *Ikeya-Seki* comet, but the Indonesian peasants had their own interpretation, it was considered a bad sign. On September 30, seven Army Generals were assassinated and for next months three millions people killed.

The Fact is 6 Army Generals in Jakarta and one in Yogyakarta assassinated, 3 million people were killed, and what does the conspiracy theory assert?

The first theory: Indonesian Communist Party (PKI) and its members like Colonel A. Latif and Colonel Oentoeng killed the Army generals in a *coup d'etat*, the outraged people revenged and kill 3 million communist members (*Sources: Soeharto regime official publications*).

The second theory: It was Soeharto plot to retaliate his dismissal as a commander of Central Java Army Division based in Semarang. In 1950's there was an organized crime in Central Java, the main activity is smuggling the main commodity like sugar, rice and soybean. The field actors were Lim Sioe Liong, Tee Kian Seng and Tik Liong; they were nicknamed the *Semarang Gang*.

Tee Kian Seng aka Bob Hasan was a cabinet member under Soeharto administration, now serving 5-year term in the Nusa "Alcatraz" Kambangan prison off shore Java mainland. Tik Liong aka Sutikno was detained and died mysteriously behind the bar a couple months after detention and before trial began.

The *Semarang Gang* another activity was embezzling the used cars belong to Central Java Army Division. The activity was so intense to catch the attention of Chief Staff of the Central Java Army Division Colonel Pranoto Reksosamodra and Lieutenant Colonel Soenaryo the chief of Military Police Corps (CPM). They investigated the crime and surprisingly they found the clues connected to then-Colonel Soeharto, the commander of Central Java Army Division.

Reksosamodra and Soenaryo reported to the Chief Staff of the Indonesian Army General Abdul Haris Nasution, he soon assigned a special task force to prosecute Soeharto; later on Soeharto was fired and reeducated in Bandung West Java. The members of the task force were Major General S. Parman, Major General MT Harjono, Brig. General Soetojo Siswomihardjo, Brig. General S. Pandjaitan, Leutenant General Ahmad Yani the Chief of Indonesian Army as a supervisor and Major General Soeprapto as chairman. They all died September 30, 1965 *coup d'etat*. Nasution survived from assassination after jumping over the fence to his next door the Iraqi embassy in the early morning, but his daughter was killed by the rebel. Who did and why? (*Source*: www.munindo.bre.de and www.xs4all.nl).

Whosoever masterminding them all, Major General Soeharto benefited from the September 1965 coup; he became a surviving general to carry on the Indonesian administration and had no rival. Later, his relatives became very wealthy.

In 1965 Pranoto Reksosamodra reunited with Soeharto in the Indonesian Army Headquarter, Jakarta. When Leutenant General Ahmad Yani was killed in the coup, President Soekarno three times called Reksosamodra to be appointed as the Acting-Chief of Indonesian Army. Each time Soekarno sent his senior staffs to call Reksosamodra they were prevented by Soeharto the Chief of Indonesian Army, Soeharto appointed himself as the Chief of Indonesian Army to replace Leutenant General Ahmad Yani.

President Soekarno called Reksosamodra over and over by sending some Army senior staffs, they were:

(1) Leutenant Colonel Infantry Ali Ebram the First-Chief of Presidential Guards,

(2) Brig. General Sutardio the Attorney General together with Brig. General Soenaryo the Chief of Intelligence Committee under the Attorney General, and

(3) Colonel Mariner Bambang Widjarnako the President's private guard (*Source*: www.megaforpresident.org).

Lim Sioe Liong aka Sudono Salim was the owner of Bank Central Asia (BCA) and the main Soeharto inner circle. He could see Soeharto anytime anywhere, so he did when Soeharto was in the Presidential Palace. Lim was wearing a short pant and T-shirt in the Presidential Palace when General Mohammad Yusuf the Joint Army Commander spotted him in 1982. Yusuf was so angry and slapped Lim; the latter complained to Soeharto and Yusuf was demanded to resign although he was one of three generals to force Soekarno to resign (two other are Panggabean and Basuki Rahmat); in fact Soeharto will be nothing without Yusuf. Anyway, Yusuf was a friend while Lim was crony.

Soeharto was forced to resign in 1998 after the students rally, the Indonesian currency was plummeting from Rp. 2,000.00 for a single US dollar to Rp. 18,000.00. The economics did not rebound even after and during three Soeharto's successors Habibie, A. Wahid and Megawati. The sporadic bomb explosions occurred almost everywhere but never being completely resolved. Even the bad news came from Bali a tourist island 800 miles east of Jakarta on October 12, 2002. The powerful bomb exploded outside two nightclubs packed with local and foreign tourists, at least 180 people dead some of them mutilated and more than 300 injured.

The number of casualties is higher than the Oklahoma bombing in 1995. The terrorists have operated in Indonesia; it was the worst terrorism in Indonesia ever since and worst one since the September 11 attacks. The United nation on October 15, 2002 issued a resolution #1438 to condemn the terrorism and urged its members to help Indonesia to fight the terrorism. The World Moslem League on October 16, 2002 also condemned the Bali explosion.

The Bali bloodbath has opened some possibilities and question of who did and what is the motive, whosoever did and whatsoever the reason it was a crime against the humanity and should be brought to justice. No single religious teaching of Buddhism, Christianity, Hindu and Islam in Indonesia justify the terrorism.

4.5. Myanmar

Myanmar is a developing country with low income per capita in Asia but has very high skill and advanced method to kill and **terrorize** the Moslems. "Authorities in Myanmar aided the killing of Rohingya Muslims last year, according to Human Rights Watch.

In a new report into the unrest, the organization said security forces either stood by or joined in as Rakhine Buddhist mobs went on the rampage, slaughtering men, women and children between June and October" (http://www.euronews.com/2013/04/22/rights-group-blames-myanmar-authorities-for-muslim-killings/).

The killing of Moslem is still continuing until May 2013; "They slept terrified in the fields, watching their homes burn through the night. And when they returned Wednesday, nothing was left but ashen debris. One day after hundreds of rampaging Buddhists armed with bricks stormed a clutch of Muslim villages in the closest explosion of sectarian violence yet to Myanmar's main city, Yangon, newly displaced Muslims were combing through the smoldering wasteland where their homes once stood, facing their losses and a suddenly uncertain future" (http://news.yahoo.com/myanmar-anti-muslim-violence-kills-1-injures-9-074322326.html).

The global silence over the Moslem killing in Myanmar suggesting that the method of attack, and not the number of victim, most probably which determined the global condemnation; if the terrorists used the bomb then they are condemned, but when they used the dagger, machete and brick then the world keeps silence because the victim deaths were quiet; while death from the explosive was heard aloud! It always unbalanced coverage by the press, if the victims are Moslems they kept silence, but if the victims are not Moslem or the suspect is Moslem then the publications are intense.

4.6. Yemen

Yemen is a tiny country in the southern part of Arab peninsula; it was the native of Abrahah who sent the troop on the elephants to destroy Ka'bah in 571 AD the year when Mohammad was born. Yemen today is a merge of two Yemenis: South and North. South Yemen was a communist government and North Yemen was a nationalist. In the late 1980 a South Yemeni special envoy came to the North Yemen, he visited the national palace; and as he opened the brief case it exploded killing the envoy and VIP of North Yemen. In 1990's two Yemenis united; some problems resolved but there are still some.

As a tradition, when a baby boy born in Yemen he will hear three kinds of sound: *azan* a call for prayer, a transaction to buy for him a new *janbiya* the traditional machete and, a Kalashnikov to celebrate the born a new knight and future leader.

The arm and explosive are common things in Yemen, when USS Cole crippled at the port of Aden on October 12, 2000 after a terrorist attack it was considered as 'a common thing', but it was not for the USA because it lost 17 mariners. In October 2002, Limburg a French tanker was attacked; the terrorists did not satisfy with the attacks on the land, they have expanded to the sea.

5. Europe

5.1. Balkan Countries

Prior to the Balkan war the Yugoslavia currency was so good, one single dinar equal to 20 US dollars more, but after the IMF 'shock therapy' the rate was so low and lead to the chaos. The similar condition occurred in Indonesia, in 1992 one single US dollar equal to 1,997. [00] Rupiahs and in 1998 the Rupiah had plummeted in value by 8 times to Rp. 16,000. [00] for every single US dollar, a super inflation similar to chaos in 1965.

There are two theories of the Yugoslavia breakup; the first: it was torn apart by the ethnic war; there was the internal diversity even since Iosif Broz Tito administration. The second: the economics fiasco after IMF 'shock therapy'. The second theory was introduced by Polyconomics; Jude Wanniski, the founder of Polyconomics wrote a memo in 1999 to then-Secretary of State Madeleine Albright reminding her about Polyconomics memo in 1993 written by Criton Zoakos a Polyconomics staff on the continuing Balkan crisis (http://www.polyconomics.com/searchbase/04-08-99.html).

The ethnic war is just a side effect of the economics collapse. The analysis is based on the currency rate before and after the external monetary intervention. No matter the main cause, the fact is more than 1,000,000 civilians killed, raped, permanently injured and fled their native land; even 8,000 Moslems have been slaughtered within a week only during the Srebrenica genocide in 1995.

The former Bosnian leader Radovan Karadzic and former Yugoslav leader Slobodan Milosevic were charged of ethnic cleansing by the International Tribunal. Karadzic was arrested in Belgrade on July 21, 2008 while Milosevic died in The Hague prison cell from the heart attack in 2006. Karadzic, Drago Nikolic, Vujadin Popovic, and Ljubisa Beara are still at large until 2003; and Milosevic was sent to The Hague for trial and died before being sentenced. Eventually, Nikolic surrendered and transferred to The Hague on March 17, 2005; he was and sentenced for 35 years. Popovic also surrendered and transferred to The Hague on April 14, 2005; he was and sentenced for life for killing the Bosnian Moslems. Beara surrendered and transferred to The Hague on October 10, 2004. The International **Criminal Tribunal for the former Yugoslavia (ICTY)** in 2010 was convinced that he committed genocide of Bosnian Moslems at Srebrenica massacre in 1995. He was convicted of genocide, extermination, murder, and persecution; and was sentenced to life in prison. They are the modern terrorists in uniform who terrorized the Balkan Moslems in 1994-1995. Thanks to the ICC and ICTY for bringing the terrorist to justice. The world is still waiting for when the Indonesian terrorists who terrorized Indonesian Moslems in several parts of Indonesian archipelago from 1976 – 2011, such as Atjeh massacre from 1976 to 2005 with 15,000 Moslem victims; Poso tragedy 2003-2007 with 770 Moslem victims; Ambon tragedy in 1995, 1998-2011 with around 400 Moslem victims would be prosecuted and brought to justice.

5.2. Chechnya: Dzhokhar Dudayev (1944-1996)

After the breakup of Soviet Union, the former satellite states which were forcibly united in the Soviet Union like Ukraine and Georgia declared the independence without interference; but when Chechnya did in 1991 the war erupted. What is the difference?

There are two analyses, firstly because Chechnya is a potential track for oil pipe, if Chechnya ruled by non-cooperative leader the Russia will get nothing; secondly because the Chechnya leader Dzhokhar Dudayev (1944-1996) was a Moslem General who was well trained during the Soviet Union era. Any analysis would be appreciated, but the fact is 800,000 civilian killed during Russian invasion since 1991. This is terrorism by state, unfortunately whenever the victims are Moslems then the press kept silence but when the actors or suspected actors were Moslems then the press widely published the news daily. This is the first massive killing after the Soviet Union breakup, Russia always filled with purge; after Lenin and Stalin now is Boris Yeltsin's turn.

Dudayev was the first Chechen native to reach the high rank in the Soviet Union Army; he resigned in 1990 to lead his native land for the freedom. He commanded his people to fight the oppressing Russia for 5 years, and a couple days before his death he and 35,000 volunteers destroyed Russian troops of 400,000 and prompting the immediate retreat from Grozny.

Dudayev was not killed in the battlefield but in his headquarter in 1996 when he was talking from his satellite phone; a sophisticated phone interceptor located his exact position and a satellite-guided missile killed him. It was the first time a satellite telephone was involved in the launching a guided missile to kill a nation leader; in fact it was a bad advertisement for the satellite phone companies. He was lured to directly talk to Yeltsin about the truce, but it was a Russian death trap: a sophisticated phone interceptor and a missile. Dudayev should have said "Nyet, comrade".

5.3. Germany: Hitler

Who is 'the champion' of killing more than one million people in the modern history? Stalin, Pol Pot or Hitler? If Hitler killed six millions, then he is, but if he killed four millions then Stalin is. The victims of Hitler terrorism are European Jews; some historian estimated six millions died and some of them said less than four million, but they did agree on the fact the Jews died from various cases of pain, injury, shooting, gas chamber, starvation and so forth.

The "search and prosecute" over the Hitler aides like Adolf Eichmann, Joseph Mengele, Papon, and others has been continuing until 2000 more than 50 years after the atrocity; and the lawsuit to recover the victims property still going on until now. It is a very long process which needs the patience and special skill, but the relatives of the victims investigated the case properly. It is a good example how to search and prosecute the criminal long time after the incident; their expertise should have been transferred to the International Prosecutor to bring the human rights abuser to justice. Their expertise deserves to raise the thumbs up.

Eichmann was arrested in Argentine, brought to Israel and sentenced to death; his dead body cremated and scattered over the sea in 1962. Mengele the butcher from Auschwitz never be found and presumed dead –maybe he was founded but was not announced like Eichmann- and Papon was released from France prison in 2002.

The holocaust during Hitler era is a subject to dispute until today. The main question is why it happened amid the modern Europe with so many civilized countries and just in front of Vatican Church, and if the Vatican knew why it was a subject to blame?

The common theory is the leaders of Catholic Church knew what Nazi did but did not care about the Jews fate just because of their own safety and their stand of anti-Semitism. That is the conclusion of Daniel Goldhagen and John Cornwell two well-known authors about the holocaust.

During World War II, Nazi created the horrible death camps in Poland and Germany such as in **A**uschwitz, **B**elzec, **C**helmo, **M**ajdanek, **S**obibor and **T**reblinka. These places were notorious with horrible sites of concentration camps to kill European Jews during Hitler reign.

5.4. Ireland

The violence clearly spread around the globe, even some of them had had the deep root dated back to a couple of centuries ago. The people are not tired to deal with the perennial violence, one after another. The violence in Ireland began five hundred years ago when King Charles of England conquered the Ireland in 1549. The tension between native Irish and Briton was getting worst when the Catholic Irish were forcefully converted by Oliver Cromwell (1599-1658) to be Anglican-Catholic or Protestantism.

The modern Irish movement against the United Kingdom started on April 1916 when Patrick Pearse announced the establishment of Irish Republic. Later, the revolutionary faction established the Irish Revolutionary Army (IRA), the tension and clash between British Army in Ireland and IRA are continuing ever since; and both sides to blame each other.

5.5. Soviet Union

"Violence can only be concealed by a lie; the lie can only be maintained by violence"; Aleksandr "Gulag" Solzhenitsyn

Vladimir Ilyich Lenin (1870-1924) was born in 1870 when the Czar ruled Russia. Lenin was an activist in Bolshevik Marxist Party, and during the1905-1907 revolution he developed the idea of the proletariat hegemony in the bourgeois democratic revolution, it was the communist revolution. He was a leader of the October Uprising against the Czar, and as the Bolshevik prevailed the Czars were assassinated, no one left behind. Lenin was elected the head of the Soviet Government on March 11, 1918.

Before his death in 1924 he told his comrades not to elect Joseph Stalin (1879-1953) as the Soviet leader, but Stalin who was ever twice exiled to Siberia in 1902 and 1913 during Bolshevik revolution was too smart to defeat. The struggle for power after the death of Lenin was so bloody and Stalin became a proletariat dictator of the USSR for a quarter century (1928-1953).

Stalin was an ambitious leader where the violence is the means to achieve the objective; the ends justify the means. To obtain the self-sufficient food for the Soviet Russia, in 1928 he launched the campaign of "kolkhoz", a collective agriculture and "the agriculture lands without border". The kolkhoz was formed from the peasant lands which were forcefully taken over by the communist party. During the bloody campaign, the millions of innocent peasant perished; and during the 1934-1938 "massive purge" another millions of "public enemies" were imprisoned or shot to death. Nevertheless, he introduced a 5-year plan for economic and industry development which adopted by Soeharto regime within his "Repelita" concept during his dictatorship in Indonesia for 32 years.

Stalin was so smart, in order to minimize the possibility of war against the multiple enemy and front, temporarily he signed a non-aggression Pact with Hitler in 1938 and involved in the international conferences after World War II in Yalta Russia and Potsdam the Netherlands. This international conference was an embryo of the United Nation, where the US President Thomas Woodrow Wilson was awarded a Nobel peace prize in 1919 for his initiative in establishing the UN.

In the other side, Stalin's efforts were not in vain since the Soviet Union to take the political control over Eastern Europe after the World War II. That was the beginning of the Cold War between the US (supported by NATO) and Soviet Union (supported by the Warsaw Pact) until 1991 when the Soviet Union collapsed as Boris Yeltsin separated Russia from the USSR. It was a long cold war stretched for five decades with so many unpublicized victims. The last USSR president Mikhail Sergeyevich Gorbachev had his choice of "perestroika" rather than continuing the cold war. He ordered the Soviet troops withdrawal from Afghanistan in May 1988, and his policy paid off when he achieved the Nobel peace prize in 1990. Stalin's live was full with terror, he had orchestrated the theft of the nuclear secret from the US which could be used to kill another millions, he was very happy when Klaus Fuchs and his wife successfully stole a bunch of nuclear documents. His legacy of Cold War was carried on by his successors Nikita Sergeyevich Khrushchev, Leonid Ilyich Brezhnev, Constantin Chernenko, and Yuri Andropov over the decades. Stalin still caused the victims even after his death.

5.6. The London Attack

The London Attack of 2013 is the killing of 25 year-old British soldier Lee Rigby by the suspects Michael Adebolajo, 28, and Michael Adebowale, 22 on May 22, 2013 on the broad daylight in the city of Woolwich, East London UK. Lee Rigby; was off-duty when he was run over by a car and stabbed with butcher knives as he was walking near his barracks.

His tragic death sparks the public condemnations including from Moslem organization inside and outside Britain. The Islamic Society of North America (ISNA) issued a special announcement supporting the British Prime Minister David Cameron who was quoted to declare that "This was not just an attack on Britain and on the British way of life. It was also a betrayal of Islam and of the Muslim communities who give so much to our country." The Muslim Council of Britain also condemned the attack and called it "a truly barbaric act that has no basis in Islam," and urged all parties the Muslims and non-Muslims "to come together in solidarity to ensure the forces of hatred do not prevail."

Both suspects to be believed as the Nigerian descendant of British citizens were shot by London police and were taken to custody after the incident. Adebolajo talked to a witness after the incident and was recorded on digital camera. The student of University of Greenwich from 2003 to 2005 before drop out; was a Christian who converted to Islam in 2004; one of his friend told the reporters that Adebolajo did not attend the Islamic lecture and other activity since two years ago. In 2007 he was photographed to march in London with his friends shouting slogans in a protest against the arrest of six people in anti-terror raids.

The reporters quoted Adebolajo's recorded reason that he killed a British soldier "…. *because Muslims are dying daily. This British soldier is an eye for an eye, a tooth for tooth*" he referred to a balanced retaliation over what British soldiers did against the Moslems; a murky reason that he did not elaborate. A witness was quoted to say "*These two guys were crazed. They were just not there. They were just animals.*" A couple minutes later, two suspects asked the bystanders to take the photographs and look to be so eager to broadcasted on TV; a true insane action on the street of London. It is not clear if this horrific action may have a possible correlation with 2008 incident; according to The Guardian newspaper, citing police and court records, that Adebowale and his two friends were stabbed in 2008 by a man in a London apartment where his 18-year-old friend died. Michael Adebolajo is one among nine suspected members of the Al-Shabaab Movement arrested by Kenyan police in 2010 when they were on the way to Somalia to fight there.

A couple hours after the incident, a man armed with two knives threw a smoke grenade into a mosque in Essex, east of London, he demanded any Moslem inside the mosque to explain the Woolwich slaying of Lee Rigby. According to the mosque's secretary the only person inside the mosque called police right away and the police quickly arrested the smoke grenade thrower. Some mosques in UK including one in Grimsby were attacked amid fears of a backlash following the killing of Lee Rigby by extremist Moslem convert. Two men were arrested by police patrolling around the Grimsby mosque, which was still attacked despite the presence of police around the area following another attack on the complex a couple of days before. The killing of Lee Rigby is committed by the Moslem personnel(s); so why the mosques as the Moslem institutions are destroyed?

No matter the reason, this killing is wrong; it is not jihad; it is terrorism since London is not battle field. The England police should have found the indoctrinator and actor intellectual of this brutal action to prevent the future terror.

6. Middle East: Shabra and Chatilla

انـا يـا قـومي أمنت بالشـعب المضيع والمكبل
فحملت رشاشي لتحمل الاجيال من بعدي مني
دين عليك دماؤنـا والدين حق لا يؤجل

Ana yaa qoumy aamantu bish-sha'bel-mudhayya'e wal-mukabbal
Fa hamiltu reshaashy letahmelal-ajyaalo min ba'dy minny
Daenon alayka demaa'ona wad-daeno haqqon laa yo'ajjal

My people
I am on the side of neglected and abused people
Then I bring my arm
Hoping the next generation will do as I did
My blood is your debt
The debt should be paid off

(A Palestinian unidentified poet wrote this poem on the Palestinian
flag; the Israeli troop found it during a raid to the Palestinian camp in
South Lebanon in early 1970's)

Menachem Begin was the Israeli Prime Minister and Ariel
Sharon was a Secretary of Defence when the pro-Israeli
Lebanese Christian militiamen on September 16, 1982 raided the
Palestinian refugee camps of Shabra and Chatilla in Lebanon
leaving about two thousand refugees died. The inquiry inside the
Israeli Defence Ministry decided that Ariel Sharon the raid
planner was "indirectly responsible" for the mass killing. The
inquiry has been prompting Sharon to resign from the Menachem
Begin administration in 1983. Since 2006 he was hospitalized for
the multiple health problems.

This chapter noted lot of violence in our civilized world; it is
obvious that not single country in the world was free from the
violence. Will we add some more for our kids?

The Blood Stained List:

#	Year	Place	Incident	Victims
1	1915	Russia, Japan	Russia-Japan War	400,000
2	1917	Russia	Bolshevik revolution	500,000

3	1930	Europe	World War I	1,300,000
4	1945	Europe	World War II	6,000,000
5	1945	Asia	World War II	3,000,000
6	1953	Soviet Union	Kolkhoz, communism, purge	5,000,000
7	1948	Palestine	Mideast War I	500,000
8	1946-1975	China	KMT-KCT Civil war	3,000,000
9	1953	Korea	Korean War	1,000,000
10	1965	Indonesia	Coup d'etat, civil war	3,000,000
11	1967	Mideast	Mideast War II	700,000
12	1973	Mideast	Mideast War III	800,000
13	1975-2000	Timor	Soeharto invaded Timor	300,000
14	1978	Cambodia	Communism and civil war	3,000,000
15	1980-1988	Iran, Iraq	Iran-Iraq war, rivalry in the gulf provoked	1,000,000
16	1982	Lebanon	Massacre of Shabra-Chatila Palestinian camps,	2,000
17	1982-2002	Sudan	Civil War	2,000,000
17	1982	Lampung	Soeharto killed Moslems	500
18	1982	Priok	Soeharto killed Moslems	1,000
19	1991	Kuwait	Gulf War	500,000
20	1992-2000	Balkan	Yugoslavia breakup	2,000,000
21	1996	Rwanda	Civil war	1,000,000
22	1996-2002	Burundi	Civil war	500,000
23	2001	USA	Terror in USA soil, two planes slammed WTC buildings in NY	2,900
24	2001-2002	India	Moslem-Hindu Riot	2,000
Total				35,508,400

More than thirty five million people died from the violence since the beginning of 20th century. The victims in Myanmar, Sri Lanka (Tamil Elam uprising), Haiti, Argentine, Chile, Bolivia, Congo, South Africa, Ivory Coast, Algiers, Ireland and Chechnya are not included yet. All victims are the loved ones in their relatives, they ever be the children with so many happiness. Maybe we do not care about the alleged abusive priests in USA, but what about the assassination of Bishop Oscar Romero of Salvador and Bishop Steven Biko of South Africa?

Tens of million people were killed and we knew who did, but nobody was brought to justice except some in Nuremberg and The Hague trials. Is there any justice in this fragile world? Some world leaders expressed the skepticism.

The World Health Organization released a report in 2002 that every 40 seconds someone commits suicide, and every 60 seconds a human being is killed. Is there any method to stop the violence by establishing an international court that will hardly sentence the violator of human rights as well as establishing the international prosecution to chase the criminals anywhere in this planet?

The act of violence is a sign of primitiveness; unfortunately it happened since the prehistoric era -when Qabel and Habel two sons of Adam involved in a dispute that had to be resolved with a tragic death- until today where we are living together in the modern civilized world. The human being and the animals have their own mechanism as well: **self-destruction mechanism**; otherwise this world will be too crowded (?).

One amongst Ten Commandments Moses conveyed to the modern civilization was "no killing anyone"; it was referring to the incident of Qabel and Habel long long time before. Torah, Bible and Qor'an reminded the human being that the killing of innocence is equal to the killing of whole mankind (**5:32**); it indicates how valuable a single life is.

Let us calculate: suppose Qabel and Habel lived 10,000 years ago. At the age of 25 the victim i.e. Habel son of Adam should had have a baby and the baby within 25 year to have a baby; two generations every 50 years and the exponent factor of Habel offspring were 200 generations.

The amount of lives lost was $2 \char`\^ 200 = 1.61E+60$ or 1,606,938,044,258,990,000,000,000,000,000,000,000,000,000,0 00,000,000,000,000,000 people. So how many zillions the lives should be if 35,500,000 victims still alive and to have the offspring?

The twentieth century is a century of bloodshed. We are lucky still alive today, we need no more violence.

Chapter Four: Understanding of Jihad

Si vis pacem para bellum. If you want the peace, prepare for war

1. Paradigm of Jihad

After learning so many violence in the previous chapter, now is the time to discuss about jihad; is it struggle or terrorism?

The Badr was the first and hard war against the coalition of disbelievers, atheists, and polytheists in Mecca and the adjacent areas. It was a decisive struggle to determine the future life of Islam; however upon returning with the victory Prophet Mohammad said to his companions "We returned from the minor *jihad*". His companions were wondering and asking: "What do you mean?" he replied: "We return from minor and simple jihad, there will be a greater one; that is jihad against ourselves" (authentic *hadith* certified by Imam Bokhary).

The term used in this narration (*hadith*) is "jihad"; the Badr was definitely a battle between life and death with so many casualties, it was a decisive battle but it was considered only as a minor battle. The "*jihad against our self*" will be greater and harder because there is no enemy but the Moslem himself. It will be a hard, steadfast and boring struggle within and by a Moslem himself.

Since the beginning the jihad has an ambivalent meaning both outward and inward, it could not be simply translated as "the holy war" as so many writers did; the major jihad is the continuous struggle against any evil inclination within Moslem himself.

The war against Soviet Union troops in Afghanistan was a perfect example of jihad -in the meaning of holy war against the disbelievers- in the modern history where some Islamic states supported it. However, this jihad became questionable as Soviet Union left Afghanistan; some scholars considered it degraded to the struggle for power. Afghanistan is worth to compete for, since it has so many natural resources which are essential for the **modern military** and **civilian living**.

The other *hadith* about jihad was narrated by Abdullah bin Mas'od, he said: *"I asked God's Messenger 'What's the best deed?' he replied 'The prayer just on time'. And I asked again 'What's next?' he replied 'To be nice and dutiful to your parents', I further asked 'What's next?' he replied 'Jihad in the path of God'"* (authentic *hadith* certified by Imam Bokhary).

The term of "jihad" is mentioned at least four times in the Qor'an (9:73, 9:88, 25:52, and 66:9) and two times in the Prophet's *hadith;* this term is open for so many translations and meanings. The original meaning of jihad in Arabic is *"to do something with full intention and capability"* as "I do this job with full intention and capability or I do jihad against myself". According to the Arabic linguistics (*ilmus-sarf*) jihad is derived from **jaahada – yojaahido – jihaadan**. Jihad is the source of Moslem spirit whether for self defense against the external threat or to spread Islam, it is **not** a justification to create the violence in any part in the world.

During the classic period of Islam history (1100 – 1300 AD), there were two popular terms related to Jihad: *Darul-Islam* and *Darul-Harb* (the Islamic state and the Enemy state). The Division of world into two categories *Darul-Islam* and *Darul-Harb* was introduced during the Crusade as a respond to the "war of cross" declared by Pope Urban II in 1095.

The clarification to distinguish *Darul-Islam* and *Darul-Harb* was very important among other thing on the relation to '*jinayat*' or Islamic Criminal Law especially in the case of involuntary manslaughter.

The law codified: *"A Mo'men a true believer shall not kill the other unless in the case of an involuntary mistake. Whosoever killed a believer by mistake; the killer should set a slave free and pay the '**diyat**' fine paid to the relative of victim unless waived. If the killer came from the country of your enemy then he should set a slave free, and if he came from the country has a truce between you and them then he should pay the 'diyat' fine paid to the relative of victim and set a slave free"* (4:92).

Darul-Islam and *Darul-Harb* are not explicitly found in the Qo'ran, the original terms are *'min qoumin aduwwin-lakom'* or *the country of your enemy* which refers to the enemy state; and *'min qoumin baynakom wa baynahom meesaq'* or *the country has a truce between you and them* which refers to a friendly state. The term of *Darul-Islam* and *Darul-Harb* was invented by the classic scholars in order to simplify the classification for the common people just in the case of a criminal act.

Today there is no Crusade and no declaration that Islam is the enemy, therefore to classify a country as *Darul-Islam* or *Darul-Harb* is not simple and most probably is not necessary because the Moslem can be found in every country in the world. To classify the USA as an enemy state is a big mistake ever, since there are seven million Moslems living and born in the country. The basic thought is to call the mankind into the ultimate truth with the wisdom and the example of good deeds, and if the discussion is necessary it should be done with good manners (not the violence and terrorism, **16:125**).

The Prophet Mohammad taught the Moslem to make the *"salatul-haajat"* a special prayer to ask God's guidance before doing something important, the preliminary study and deep discussion with some *fiqh* books as the reference should be performed; no such action will be cleared unless the obvious guidance is coming. He also taught with every example how to call the mankind to Islam peacefully, when he had to face the enemy he brought his men outside the populated city to avoid the civilian casualty. When he won a war he did not make a 'killing field', and when he captured the POWs he ordered his men to treat them accordingly (**76:8-10**, see Chapter Five: The Conquest of Mecca and Chapter Six: The Ethics of War).

In the classic period there was a dispute between the common people about the status of Abyssinia (ancient Ethiopia); was it *Darul-Islam* or *Darul-Harb*. The King of Abyssinia Najhase was embracing Islam upon the arrival of Mohammad, but he let his people to choose their own. The official stance of Najhase was to welcome Mohammad and his migrating companions, he was a wise king; the stability of the nation was his primary concern as well as the religion. Najhase had been trying to make a balance between his administration and his people; it was a matter of the public policy.

Abyssinia was not an Islamic state but it never opposed Islam. Therefore, any consideration that put Abyssinia in the *Darul-Harb* category will be absolutely wrong.

The case of Abyssinia in 615 AD is similar to the case of USA today where more than 7 million Moslems live. The USA never prevented the spread of Islam and never declared the war against Islam. President George W. Bush in a visit to Washington Grand Mosque after 9/11 said: "Islam is a religion of peace".

The September 11, 2001 attack was a tragedy for the mankind and a big loss for the USA and Moslems. Whosoever the plotter(s) of September 11 attacks they knew nothing about the Islamic Law and the ethics of Islamic war. May God protect us from the future tragedy; God Bless America.

The reference to justify the killing of the innocence people such as the casualties of 9/11 is never be available in the Islamic bibliography, and Mohammad the Prophet never provided even a single example of killing the innocence. No matter the reason and motive, and no matter who did, the 9/11 is absolutely wrong. The Moslems need more public relation and political lobby not the violence to carry on the peaceful mission as taught by Mohammad (**16:125**).

The violence against anybody whether Moslem or non-Moslem is strictly forbidden. In the past history of Islam, unfortunately, there were some wars or even the atrocity between Moslems themselves triggered by the rivalry to reach the power and not for the cause of God.

The Karbala atrocity, the war during the transfer of power from the Omayyad to the Abbasids, and Iraq-Iran war were the real examples. The Moslems, especially their leaders, should have understood that the killing another Moslem intentionally would be charged by God as committing an unforgivable sin. *"And whosoever intentionally kills a single believer, his recompense is the Hellfire to abide therein forever, and the Wrath and the Curse of God are upon him and the grand punishment is prepared for him"* (**4:93**).

If two groups of Moslems fight each other, the third party should have intervened rather than supporting one side of them; and if after the intervention there is a group which do not comply with the truce then the Moslems have to punish the defector. *"And if two parties amongst the Believers fought each other, then make the peace between the both. Anyway, if one of them outrages against the other then you all should fight against the defectors until they comply with the command of God. If they obey then make the reconciliation between the both on the basis of justice and impartiality. Verily, God loves those who are doing the wisdom (**49:9**)"*. This is the Islamic guideline whenever the conflict between Moslems erupted. The Iran-Iraq inter-Moslem war (1978-1986), the assassination of Egypt President Anwar Sadat (1981), the Gulf War (1990-1991), and the Arab Spring which eventually lead to the Syrian civil war were the fighting between Moslems themselves with so many casualties and expenses. It's the clear proof on how obtuse the Moslems today are, so the outsider easily makes them fight each other. It was not clear who did intervene, and if there was an intervention and intermediation it was not also clear who did defy. Meanwhile Russia helps Syrian government with the arms as the European countries do to the rebel groups. This is a perfect description on the situation where *"the Moslems are alike the bubble on the sea"*, unfortunately the Moslem themselves are not realizing how devastating the situation is.

No violence and war allowed during the sacred months, but the combat against a rebellion or armed uprising that happened inside the *Masjidil-Haram* (Holy Mosque) of Mecca during the sacred month in 1979 was permissible because three reasons: (a) the rebel violated the prohibition of fight in the sacred months, (b) to subdue the armed rebellion against the Islamic state and (c) to restore the order.

Everybody has his/her own rights for freedom, but the non-Moslem leaders cannot insult Mohammad the last Prophet as did Evangelist Franklin Graham, Evangelist Pat Robertson, Evangelist Jerry Falwell, and the Qor'an burning by the order of Pastor Terry Jones at Dove Church, Florida (https://www.youtube.com/watch?v=XDmaFehshys) on March 20, 2011. The Moslem scholars never ever insulted Jesus (Isa), Moses, David and other Messengers, why the Evangelists did? Although the American Evangelists insulted Mohammad, the Moslem scholars considered that what the Evangelists did is their personal business not the government's one.

The declaration of 'holy war' in 1095 was a different case; the Crusade declared by Pope Urban II incited the anarchy and consecutive war with the simultaneous victory for two parties for almost 100 years with hundreds of thousand casualties and billions of dollars lost. It was the bitter past history just because of a single person; we are confident no such case will happen in the future.

Prophet Mohammad decreed to the Moslems to hold tightly on the Qor'an and Hadith otherwise the Moslems will be lost, and in another decree he said: "**Someday the Moslems will be like the bubble on the sea**", when the companions asked him if in that time the Moslems are minority, he answered "**Definitely not, you are majority but you loved the worldly prosperity so much and you afraid of the death**". The Moslem scholars have some interpretations concerning this hadith some of them presume the predicted time has come.

Today most Moslems love the money so much; they sold the unlawful (haram) products and benefited from them. The Moslem parents prefer to send their children to the public schools -where the religious practices are not available due to the doctrine to spare between state and religion- rather than send them to the private Moslem schools because they do not want to spend more money. The impact of their decision is their children do not know how to pray properly specially the Friday prayer because they never had the time to do; they are still in the classroom, and even they do not know the simple daily habit: *Istinja,* the art of cleaning the body in preparation for prayer.

Now, in some US cities, the weekend Islamic Schools are available to add-up the religious teaching they miss during attending the public school. The public or private school is the matter of the parent free choice, it is freedom for everybody, but how about the religious practice like the Qor'an recitation; can our children read it or can they make a proper *sala*t and perform a right *istinja* as well?

Today is the right time for Moslems to do internal "*jihad against ourselves*" to fight against the evil preference inside, it is the best thing to do first before "*jihad*" against someone else. Can we understand if a Moslem married to four women or more instead of giving the charity to the orphans; or what is the common sense of a Moslem who does not drink the alcoholic beverage but to sell it? When the time for prayer comes some Moslem businessmen prefer to be with their business rather than going to the mosque or to make prayer just on time in their work place. The Moslem parents are busy with their jobs and businesses and do not have time to teach daily prayer to their own children. Are they going to do jihad against non-Moslem, or it is a time to do internal jihad against themselves?

The Abraham descendants including Moslems, Jews, and Christians would be far from the truth whenever they neglect the prayer and to follow the lust (**19:59**). It is the time for them all to repent and back to the religion because the life is very short, a day in the Hereafter is equal to 1,000 world years (**32:5**). There is a frightening verse in Surah Al-Anfal of the Qor'an; it is about a threat to punish all Moslems without exception including the pious ones whenever they let a person amongst them to perform the sin while nobody stops him. *"And fear the affliction and punishment which does not affect the sinners amongst you merely"* (**8:25**). America appreciates the religious freedom, nobody prohibits the religious practices in the USA; the Moslems prohibit themselves.

To put remark of "terrorist" on Islam and Moslem in general is not fair since every religion has its own extremist and terrorist who misunderstood their own religion and put an extreme interpretation over their religious teachings. Islam has Osama bin Laden, Christian has David Koresh and Timothy McVeigh; and Judaism has Irv Rubin. To make it clear, everybody knows OBL who was killed during the US Navy Seal operation in Pakistan on May 2, 2011, yet for McVeigh and Rubin it is necessary to elaborate in brief.

McVeigh was a 33-year old American terrorist who was convicted of using the weapon of mass destruction to bomb the Alfred Murrah Federal Building in Oklahoma City on April 19, 1995 which killed 168 innocent people and injured more than 800 people. McVeigh did his action for the retaliation against US government who raided the David Koresh's Christian Temple of Waco Texas in 1993 with 86 casualties including 4 US government agents. McVeigh was executed in June 11, 2011.

Irv Rubin was a 57-year old Chairman of Jewish Defense League; he was officially charged of Federal terrorism, attempting to blow up a Moslem mosque in Culver City California and the office of Republican Congressman Darrell Issa. Rubin fell to his death from a 20-foot-high railing; it's presumed a suicide, in Los Angeles Metro Detention Center in November 13, 2002 while awaiting his trial.

We may not put the blame of McVeigh's action on Christianity and Christian people; we may not put the blame of Irv Rubin's action on Judaism and Jewish people as we may not put the blame of Osama bin Laden's action on Islam and Moslems in general.

2. The Qor'an and Arabic

The Qor'an is the official source of jihad, to understand what the jihad is; the Moslem should have understood the Qor'an first to prevent the deviation of meaning. The Qor'an is a compilation of the revelations from God conveyed by Gabriel the Angel to Mohammad the last Messenger. It was revealed in the eloquent Arabic with so complicated but perusal rule, idiom, grammar, literature, different articulation, and semantic understanding. The Qor'an Arabic is quite different from common Arabic in the Arab world today; it is not easy to understand even for the people who were born in the Middle East countries, and it differs from the common language spoken by the Arab majority.

Mohammad was illiterate; this fact gave the strong evidence that the Qor'an was not his writing. Each time he received the revelation he memorized it and called his secretary to write down on the bone, leather, dates leaf, and tablets. His secretaries were Ali bin Abu Taleb, Osman bin Affan, Obay bin Ka'ab, Zaed bin Tsabit and Moawiyya; they were requested to memorize gradually what they wrote during more than 22 years.

During Abu Bakr administration there was a battle to restrain the rebels who turned their backs to be the disbelievers; 70 companions who memorized whole Qor'an were killed in this battle. This situation encouraged Abu Bakr to compile the Qor'an from various sources and he appointed Zaed bin Tsabit as the main compiler. Zaed bin Tsabit collected the verses written on the bones, leathers, dates leaves, tablets and he made inquiries to another companions as well.

When Osman bin Affan succeeded Abu Bakr as the second Caliph he went on the compilation of Qor'an and established the Board of Compilation, he appointed Zaed bin Tsabit as chairman. The members of the Board were Abdullah bin Zobeir, Saed bin Ass, and Abdurrahman bin Haris. The board completed the writing of five copies of the compiled Qor'an, four of them were distributed to Mecca, Syria, Basra and Kofah, and the other one remained in the Capital Medina; in the next period the Moslem wrote another copies from these five.

When Moslems ruled Spain in the twelfth century they interacted with another nation and religion; the interaction lead Robert of Ketton in 1143 to translate Qor'an into the Latin language for being used in the Monastery of Clugny. From this first translation then other translations were made in some languages like Germany in 1616, French by Du Ryer in 1647, Russian in 1776, and English by Alexander Ross in 1649. These translations were secondary because they were not translated directly from Arabic but from the Latin version.

The English contemporary translation of Qor'an prepared by Muhammad Marmaduke Pickthall and Abdullah Yusuf Ali; two prominent translators who translated Qor'an directly from the Arabic. Pickthall an English Moslem translated Qor'an into English in 1930 under the title of "*The Meaning of the Glorious Koran*"; this version achieved a recommendation from Egypt scholars. Abdullah Yusuf Ali's "*The Holy Qor'an, Text Translation and Commentary*" prepared in 1934; these two translations had been printed so many times until now and well known in the Moslem countries.

Now, the various translations are done, the Saudi Arabia Kingdom prints Qor'an and the Translation in some languages and to distribute them free for the Moslem countries. Yet, a fact should have been recognized there was never being a perfect translation due the complication of Qor'an Arabic.

The Qor'an was not compiled on the basis of the revelation chronology, but on the *Taoqeefy* a decree conveyed by Gabriel the Angel, the first page of the Qor'an is not the first verse revealed. The Qor'an consists of 114 *Surahs*, 30 parts, 60 *hezbs*, 240 quarters, and 554 *roku^s*. This system makes easy for the Moslem to memorize the whole Qor'an. A Moslem used to memorize Qor'an within seven years during the childhood and another seven years to understand the meaning of Qor'an including the grammar, linguistic, semantic meaning and the knowledge related to the Qor'an.

The Qor'an 2:7 gave the warning to the people to be careful to understand it because there are some *mutashabihaat* (controversial meanings) verses like *"Yadu-llaahi faoqa aydeehem"* or **The Hand of God is over their hands**. Does God have the hands like we do? The answer of this question must be "No", because the creature must be different with The Creator. This *mutashaabihaat* verse "the Hand of God" should be translated as the Power of God.

The Qor'an was revealed in the eloquent Arabic (**12:2**), and there are so many complicated rules and parts of grammar in Arabic, some of them are:

2.1. The "Sarf"; it is a rule concerning the verb transformation in the various tenses. Unlike English; the Arabic differentiates the verb prefix for the different gender; there are some examples:

Past Tense	Present Tense (He)	Present Tense (She)	Imperative (He)	Gerund	Meaning
Qatala	Yaqtulo	Taqtulo	Oqtol	Qatl	Killing
Qaatala	Yuqaatilo	Tuqaatilo	Qaatil	Qetaal	War
Jaahada	Yujaahedo	Tujaahedo	Jaahed	Jihaad	Struggle, war, fight

The transformation from a single verb "kataba" or to write into the present tense is so complicated as follows:

Infinitive verb/past	He	Two Men	The Men	She	Two Ladies
Kataba	yaktobo	yaktobaane	Yakto-boona	taktobo	Taktobaane

Infinitive verb	The Ladies	You (man)	Me (lady/gent)	We
Kataba	yaktobna	taktobo	aktobo	Naktobo

The transformation from a single verb "*kataba*" (to write) and "*ja'ala*" (to make) into the past tense maybe 'easier':

Infinitive verb	He	They (two gents)	They (the gents)	She
Kataba	kataba	Katabaa	Kataboo	Katabat
Ja'ala	Ja'ala	Ja'alaa	Ja'aloo	Ja'alat

Infinitive verb	Two Ladies	They (ladies)	I	We
Kataba	katabataa	katabna	katabto	katabnaa
Ja'ala	Ja'alataa	Ja'alna	Ja'alto	Ja'alnaa

2.2. The "Nahw", it is the rule to pronounce the last letter of the nouns and verbs within a sentence. A verb or a noun will be pronounced in the different ways according to the function and status in the sentence; there are some examples:

The Phrase and Meaning (Nouns)	Last Letter Pronunciation	Status
Haazehe shajaraton (this is a tree)	--ton	*Rafa'*, neutral *)
Haataane shajarataane (these are two trees)	--taane	*Rafa'*
Haazehe shajaraaton (these are the trees)	--aton	*Rafa'*
Ra'eto shajaratan (I saw a tree)	--tan	*Nasb, or accusative*
Ra'eto shajaratain (I saw two trees)	--tain	*Nasb for two*
Ra'eto shajaraatin (I saw the trees)	--atin	Plural

85

		Nasb
Marartu be shajaratin (I passed by a tree)	--tin	*Jarr, or defensive*
Marartu be shajaratain (I passed by two trees)	--tain	*Jarr for two*
Marartu be shajaraatin (I passed by some trees)	--atin	*Plural Jarr*

*) Rafa' is "original stance", and there are 9 different ways to pronounce a single word "shajara".

Most nouns are pronounced "*nasb*" or accusative when their standings are objects, but the present tense verbs should be pronounced "*nasb*" whenever they are preceded by one amongst four "*nasb letters*" as "***an-lan-idzan-kay***". See how complicated this phrase is:

The Phrase and Meaning (Verbs)	Verb Changes	Status
Taktobo (you write)	--bo (M)	Single Rafa' a neutral position *)
*Arjoo **an** taktoba* (I hope you to write)	--ba (M)	Single Nasb or accusative
*Arjoo **an** taktobaa* (I hope both of you to write)	--baa (M)	Nasb for two
*Arjoo **an** taktoboo* (I hope you guys to write)	--boo (M)	Plural Nasb
Taktobeena (you write)	--beena (F)	SingleRafa' **)
Arjoo an taktobna (I hope you the ladies to write)	--bna (F)	Plural Nasb'

*) Four first lines are for the gents
**) Fifth line and the next are for ladies; M = male, F = female

The failure to pronounce the word perfectly with vowel, diphthongs or consonant may cause the change of meaning. The famous example is verse 50 of Surah Al-Baqarah "*O sons of Israel, remember when We split the sea for you, then We saved you and drowned Pharaoh (and his) people while you were looking at them*". The original text is "*Wa idz faraqnaa*" with long "*naa*" means "when We (God) split", if the word of "*faraqnaa*" is short-pronounced as "*na*" then the meaning becomes "when the ladies split". It is an extreme deviation of meaning.

2.3. The *Balaaghah*, it is a part of Arabic concerning to good rhythm and good nuance in the paragraph. The Balaaghah consists of two parts:

2.3.1. *Bayaa*n, it is dealing with the clarity of expression both spoken and written.

2.3.2. *Ma'any*, it does regulate the way to formulate the paragraph and to keep the meaning clear and no distortion or deviation therein.

The good example is in Surah Al-Baqarah verse 104 when a group of the disbelievers so eager to fabricate the new phrase for the believers. The believers used to say "***raa'enaa***" means "please listen to us, or please take care of us" to the Prophet Mohammad, then the disbelievers transformed it into and pronounced as "***ru'unah***"; it does mean "too fool".

"*Raa'enaa*" and "**ru'unah**" have a similar pronunciation but with a quite different meaning. Upon this insult, God told the Moslems to change the phrase into "onzornaa" with the same meaning, *O you the believers, say not "Raa'enaa", but say "onzornaa"; and there is painful torment available for the pagans (kaafirien)* (**2:104**).

3. *Tafsier*, the explanation

The Tarsier means "the translation and explanation". A *"mofassier"* or translator needs to know the *"mofradaat"* or the vocabulary, Nahw, Sarf (grammar) and Balaaghah (beautiful composition) before translating any verse in the Qor'an.

The knowledge of abrogated verse is very important in Tafsier since –according to some scholars- there is an abrogated verse to implement in a certain condition while the verses itself remains intact. This is the opinion of the *"Jomhorul-Mufassereen"* or the Majority of Translators. The famous example of the abrogated verse is verse 217 of Surah Al-Baqarah and its abrogation is verse 36 of Surah At-Taobah (see detail in Chapter Five: The War). The other scholar considers that both verses are valid and no abrogation because verse 217 of Surah Al-Baqarah explains the prohibition of war during the sacred months (i.e. *Moharram, Rajab, Zolqa'dah* and *Zolhijjah* months of Islamic calendar). On the other side, verse 36 of Surah At-Taobah is an explanation and a permit to a war during the sacred months under a specific circumstance if the Moslems are attacked first. Therefore the nature of prohibition for a war mentioned in verse 217 of Surah Al-Baqarah is still valid; no single Moslem will be allowed to go to a war during the sacred months unless there is an attack against the Moslems first.

There are two domains in Tafsier: the *"manqool"* and the *"ijtehaad"*. The *"Tafsier manqool"* is a translation of a verse in Qor'an based on another verse; or translating a verse with a decree (hadith) of Mohammad. The example is translating verse 217 of Surah Al-Baqarah with verse 36 of Surah At-Taobah, and the example of translating a verse with a decree (hadith) of Mohammad is the verse 238 of Surah Al-Baqarah "**Maintain your prayers especially the *middle prayer***". What is the meaning of "middle prayer"? The Moslems have to do five obligatory prayers in a day, which one is the "middle"; Mohammad explains that "middle prayer" is the afternoon prayer (*'asr*).

The other example is the meaning of "greatest pilgrimage" in verse 3 of Surah At-Taobah *"And this is the declaration from God and His Messenger to the mankind on the day of greatest pilgrimage that God and His Messenger are free from all obligations to the polytheists. So if you are the polytheists wish to repent, that is better for you, but if you turn away, then see that you cannot escape from the punishment of God. Mohammad, give the warning of a very painful torment to the pagans (kafaroo)"*. Upon the inquiry from Ali bin Abu Taleb, Mohammad said: *"The greatest pilgrimage is the day of cattle sacrifice (yom-nahr)"*.

The other domain of Tafsier is "Tafsier ijtehaad". It is the translation of Qor'an based on the knowledge and logic after fulfilling the requirements for translation. The example of Tafsier ijtehaad is the meaning of a word "toor" (mount) in verse 63 of Surah Al-Baqarah when God reminds the sons of Israel that they had have the agreement to obey God.

"And O the children of Israel; remember when We took covenant and We raised "the toor" (mountain) above you, (in that occasion God says): 'Hold tightly what We have given to you, and remember which is therein so you may become the pious people'". Abdullah bin Abbas a prominent companion and the first generation of the Moslem (*sahaba*) translated and understood "the toor" as the Mount of Toor (Mount Sinai), while **Mojahed** the second generation of the Moslem (*tabe'in*) translated it as the mount. Any mount God decided and nobody new exactly but God, Moses, and the sons of Israel who attended the convention of *"Ten Commandments"*.

4. *Hadith* and *Mostalah-Hadith*, the Prophet Tradition

Imam Bokhary went almost one hundred miles from his native village to see a scholar he heard to have a note of an action done by Mohammad the Prophet, Imam Bokhary was so eager to include the scholar's note in his book as a valid *hadith* (tradition, decree) originated from the Prophet Mohammad.

When Imam Bokhary arrived and met the scholar outside of his home, he saw the scholar was holding something in his fingers calling his chickens for food; but as the chickens were coming to him he opened his fingers and nothing inside. Imam Bokhary considered this small incident as the fraudulence and semi-lying, he said goodbye and never asked about hadith from the scholar. Imam Bokhary was sure if someone ever lied even to the chickens then how come to quote a hadith about the Prophet from a lying narrator. This is the core of the *Mustalah-Hadith* knowledge i.e. the art to decide the authentic narration from the Prophet Mohammad.

"The eggplant is the natural medicine for every disease" was another example. This *hadith* was so popular in the classic era until Imam Bokhary investigation. He asked the man "Who did narrate this *hadith*", the man said he heard it from Flan, Bokhary went to Flan and asked him from whom he heard it. Flan said he heard it from a businessman, and then Bokhary went to the businessman and asked him from whom he heard it; the businessman said he could not remember who told him. Bokhary concluded that the businessman fabricated a fake *hadith* to support his business; he was a successful eggplant merchant. Therefore the scholars considered Bokhary's book "*The Sahih*" was the second certified book after the Qor'an.

5. *Asbaabun-Nozool*, the cause of revelation

When Prophet Mohammad still alive, his companions used to directly ask him if there was any problem happened. Haulah Bint Salabah's husband one day said that her back looked like his mother's; upon the incident she realized that his husband Obada Bin Samit had to divorce her because that was the ancient Arab tradition of "*Jaheleyyah*" (the Ignorant Time). She still loved him, and she filed the petition to Prophet Mohammad, he said to wait because no such verse available yet. A couple days later God revealed him the verses in a *Surah* named "the Plaintiff Lady" (58:1-4).

Even a couple years after Mohammad passed away where so many companions still alive, there was an embarrassing incident of understanding and implementing a verse. Under the administration of second Caliph Omar bin Khattab, Qodama was appointed as the governor of Bahrain. Qodamah was a hero in the battle of Badr, Ohod and Khandaq he was a close companion of Prophet Mohammad, nobody distrust his integrity and piety. But, another Prophet Mohammad's companion named Jarod was spotting Qodama to drink the alcoholic beverage and got drunk while it was forbidden by Islamic law, then he reported the incident to Omar bin Khattab the supreme leader of Moslems in Medina.

Upon this report, bin Khattab called Qodama to the capital for the investigation; Qodama admitted to drink the alcoholic beverage and was intoxicated. As Omar started the legal proceeding, Qodama defended himself and maintained his innocence by referring to verse 93 of Surah Al-Ma'edah.

He quoted this verse: *"No sin for those who believe (in God and His Messenger) and perform the good deeds for what they ate (and drank) in the condition they keep fearing to God and believing in Him and doing the righteous good deeds; and again still fear to God and once again still fear to God and do the good deeds. God loves the good people"* (**5:93**).

The court was shaking, then bin Khattab said to the assembly "If there is any expert or witness to refute, please stand up". Upon this request Abdullah bin Abbas a prominent companion of Mohammad came to refute defendant's argument. He said: "The verse that Qodama was referring in fact is an excuse for those who passed away before the verse 90 of Surah Al-Ma'edah was revealed. *'O you the believers, verily the alcoholic beverage, the gambling, sacrifice to the idol, and lucky draw are Satan's dirty playing; so strictly avoid them hopefully you will be victorious'*. Upon the revelation of Al-Ma'edah verse 90 then the alcoholic beverages were strictly prohibited ever since **(5:90)**.

The verse 93 of Surah Al-Ma'edah revealed as the answer on the inquiry by some Mohammad's companions concerning his uncle Hamza bin Abdul-Mutalib a martyr who died in the battle of Ohod. He and another martyrs used to consume the alcoholic beverage in the past, were they sinners and would be sent to the Hellfire while they were the heroes? Upon this inquiry, God revealed the answer to Mohammad in **(5:93)**.

This is "Asbaabun-Nozool" or the knowledge of the history and context of revelation. If a prominent companion like Qodama could be wrong, so what about the common people, can they understand the exact meaning of jihad?

6. Fiqh and Osol-fiqh, Islamic Law and its basics

The insipid Islamic knowledge leads to spontaneous bad actions, a discussion is always open, but the Fiqh and Osol-fiqh should be implemented first as a means of consideration before action. Islam, like all divine religions, would never be wrong but the Moslems like other followers of divine religions can be.

The Fiqh is the knowledge about the Islamic Law. There are three domains in the Fiqh: *Ibadat* or the obligations, *Moamalat* or the social interaction, and *Jinayat* or the criminal law.

The command of ablution (wodho') could be found in the Qor'an but what its status; is it obligatory or voluntary? The knowledge of ablution status in the relation with prayer is very critical since the prayer without ablution is void. The rationale is "if an obligatory practice in the religion is void without something then something is obligatory, too". Therefore the scholars concluded that the status of ablution is obligatory not voluntary. This rationale is named *Osol-Fiqh*, and from this stance the status of other actions including the jihad in any situation could be determined. For this point of view it is very clear that the 9/11 attacks should have never ever happened if the plotter understood the *Fiqh* (Islamic Jurisprudence) and *Osol-Fiqh*.

Here is another rationale in the Osol-Fiqh:

1. "If something is considered controversial and bad then chose to avoid it"

2. "If you have to chose between two bad things then chose one with the least risk". This rationale had been surprisingly implemented in the US administration to decide an important case (see Chapter Two: Iran-Iraq).

3. "Anything considered as prerequisite for an obligation then it is also an obligation"

4. "The command of an obligation is the command of its prerequisite"

5. "The command of doing something after its prohibition is a voluntary, not obligatory."

6. "Every God's command is obligatory unless the other status was found".

This rationale within Islamic Jurisprudence was invented and attributed to Imam Shafei whose genealogy matches to the forefather of Prophet Mohammad.

7. Ijma and Qiyas, the convention and jurisprudence

Abu Bakr the first Caliph declared the war against the people who did not pay the "*zakat*" (obligatory charity) because it is a public obligation; that was the first war after Mohammad passed away. Mohammad never declared the war against them because the focus was to call the people to "*tawhed*", the oneness of God. The scholars considered Abu Bakr declaration of war against the defectors as "*ijma*" or the consensus on the Islamic law.

Abu Bakr was a generous companion, during the Tabok War where the summer was coming and the logistic for the Moslem army was not available. He donated all his wealth including tools, cattle and foods; his action made Mohammad so surprised and asked "What's left behind for your family", Abu Bakr replied "God and His Messenger".

The "*qesas*" law is a court sentence based on the equality; it is the part of '*jinayat*' or Islamic Criminal Law. If a Moslem killed another Moslem by mistake in an involuntary manslaughter case, the killer should pay the fine and set a slave free (**5:92**). The law was intended to gradually abolish the slavery and to restore the order, but now no more slavery so the sentence should be referring to the existing jurisprudence; that is "*qiyaas*" or comparison with the previous verdict in the Islamic Law. Both *ijma* and *qiyas* are the resources of Islamic Law; they are the field where the Moslem scholars maintain the contemporary law in the Islamic society.

8. Reckless Edict

An *Aleem* or cleric or religious leader in Islam has the power of issuing the religious edict or fatwa. The fatwa is a decision a Moslem scholar issued for the Moslems to do or not to do a certain thing. The right fatwa has to be followed by the Moslem since it is mandatory; before issuing the fatwa, the religious leader has to follow a strict guidelines which already codified by the previous Moslems scholar majority (*Jumahur-Olama*).

The requirements to issue a fatwa including but not limited to these rules:

(1) A fatwa is not issued to change the Five Islamic Pillars (Confession, Prayer, Charity, Ramadan fasting; and pilgrimage to Mecca).

(2) A fatwa is not issued to change Six Islamic Beliefs (in God, the Angels, Holy Scriptures, Messengers, Judgment day, Pre-destiny).

(3) The Moslem scholar who is issuing the fatwa is competent: he is not insane, not under the influence of alcohol, adult/mature, and free.

(4) The Moslem scholar who is issuing the fatwa already memorized the whole Qor'an or at least all verses related to the Islamic jurisprudence; they are around 1,000 verses within 114 Chapters/Surah.

(5) The Moslem scholar who is issuing the fatwa already memorized the whole abrogated verses in the Qor'an.

(6) The Moslem scholar who is issuing the fatwa already memorized the whole historical events related to the revelation of verses in the Qor'an (*Asbaabun-Nozool*).

(7) The Moslem scholar who is issuing the fatwa already memorized the whole Prophet Mohammad's decree (*hadist*) or at least all hadist related to the Islamic jurisprudence; they are around 1,000 hadist which were written in Imam Bokhary's "Sahih" (around 400,000 hadist), and in Imam Moslem's "Sahih" (around 300,000 hadist).

Anyway, today the Moslems tend to forget the aforementioned prerequisite and just issuing edict casually like spitting in any place and any time. The edict of Sheikh Mohammad al-Shanar a Saudi cleric over the ban for the Saudis to travel to Dubai, is one among the popular reckless fatwa ever issued by an unripe, immature, and inexperienced "Sheikh". He issued his fatwa through his Twitter account. Unfortunately, a couple of days later he retracts his edict; a perfect example of a reckless fatwa.

Is Sheikh Qardhawi's fatwa **to wage jihad** in Syria is also a reckless fatwa? He has every right to topple Bashar Assad for the political reason, it is politics not religion; but to issue the religious edict concerning jihad is another thing.

Prophet Mohammad 1434 years ago already warned of any reckless edict when he said to his companions as narrated by **Abdullah bin Amr bin Al-As** *"I heard Prophet Mohammad said 'Verily, God does not take the knowledge away by snatching it from the people, instead He takes it away by taking the religious scholars away (with their deaths) until there is no more credible religious scholar; and then the people would appoint the ignorant/reckless scholars. Whenever they are asked (about the religious case); they would issue the religious edict without a proper knowledge; and then they go astray and make the people go astray'"* (Hadist #1392 of Imam Nawawy's "Riyadhus-Salihin" quoting Imam Bokhary's and Imam Moslem's "Sahih").

9. Arab Spring and Syrian Jihad

Arab Spring is the revolutionary mass demonstration, protest, riot, and civil war with the sole intention to change the existing government in the Arab countries especially in Tunisia, Libya, Yemen, Egypt, Bahrain, to Syria. In some countries the people successfully depose the existing ruler and in some countries they are unsuccessful. Arab Spring started in Tunisia in 2010 after the death of a young Tunisian **Mohammed Bouazizi** protesting the injustice and humiliation since his merchandise was confiscated in December 2010.

Bouazizi set himself on fire on December 17, 2010 as a protest against the injustice he suffered from; he died a couple weeks later on January 4, 2011. The magnitude of his death rolls over eastward like tsunami which is sweeping and devastating the strong regimes from Zein Al-Abedeen in Tunisia, Kaddafi of Libya, Hosni Mubarak in Egypt, Ali Abdullah Saleh of Yemen to Bashar Assad in Syria within 2 years.

The turmoil in Tunisia lasts only in a year to depose Zein Al-Abedeen, one year to kill Gaddafi, one year to abdicate Saleh, another one year to topple Mubarak, but it need more that two years trying to depose Bashar Assad and now it is erupting to be a bloodiest civil war in Arab history which is still going on until June 2013.

The significance of Syrian Civil War in this book –which was not discussed in the first edition of 2002— is the use of **jihad** terminology to try to topple Bashar Assad administration. The **jihad** terminology was never used during the deposing of Zein Al-Abedeen, Gaddafi, Saleh, and Mubarak. However, as the world knew, Bashar Assad was legitimately elected a Syrian President two times after the death of his father Hafez Assad. The wage of jihad as a holy war was only permitted under a *shariah* edict and a unanimous decision by the board of Moslem scholars. There is a tight rule to impose such a jihad; it is a big question if the target of jihad is the fellow Moslem. The Moslem scholars unanimously agreed upon jihad only for the non-Moslem combatants attacking the Moslem community. Anyway, Sheikh Qardhawi; an Egyptian cleric who is on the side of Syrian rebels could have an opinion that Bashar is NOT a Moslem; therefore jihad is permissible against him. Wait a minute. If Bashar is not a Moslem, how come the Syrian Moslems overwhelmingly voted for a non-Moslem leader in 2000 and 2007? This logic is now put upside down as the bloodshed among Arabs is going on and on and on without any sign to recede; the tally in early June 2013 was 93,000 people dead.

Any people have the rights to change their administration on their preference, but using **jihad** in the pure political movement is another thing; the use of jihad to justify the killing of political adversary is an abuse of religious teaching.

Can we understand that chopping a walking man at a London street, detonating a bomb at a marathon event, bombing the mosque, and killing people in a busy market are the kind of jihad?

The effort of Syrian rebels to depose Bashar Assad is a dynamic power struggle which happens anywhere even had happened since day one of the pass of Prophet Mohammad 14 centuries ago. The use of jihad terminology in Syrian power struggle is a misrepresentation; and the call for jihad issued by Sheikh Qardhawi is a personal opinion which does not represent the majority of Moslem scholars. Bashar Assad might be dead wrong and has to be deposed, but the effort to topple him is a pure political movement as a continuation of Arab spring, it's a civil war and not a religious war which was well-known as jihad. Every civil war is alike burning a castle down after a dispute between a family members; the winner would be awarded the charcoal, and the looser would be presented the ash. It's too sad; the Moslems do not know the true meaning of jihad today, even a lot of them can not read the Qor'an a main source of jihad.

Both side, either Bashar regime or the Syrian rebels are backed up by the opposing clerics who are claiming to base their stance on the Qor'an the Moslem Holy Book. Bashar regime was supported by Sheikh Hassan Nasrallah and the Syrian rebels are supported by Sheikh Qardhawi.

Syria Civil War is floating up some unprecedented phenomenon. The belligerents may switch position in the opposite side just in matter of days. What they perceive as an "enemy" would be a "collaborator" in another time. The border between Moslems and non-Moslems became blurred; Sheikh Qardhawi names them *"thoghut"* which means Satan or idol, each side used the religious symbol to apply in the practical politics. The prophecy that the Moslems are alike the bubble on the sea has really come today, right here, right now before our eyes yet they are happy to kill each other without a single second to contemplate that this turmoil might be generated sophistically by a group outside Moslems who are so eager to see the Moslems to kill each other every day to drain the Moslems up, so no any power left behind to engage with the education, science, social welfare, brotherhood, etc.

Both Nasrallah and Qardhawi should have brought reconciliation instead of inciting more war and bloodshed. Their influences were misused in the bloodiest Arab Civil War ever.

To simplify the understanding of Syrian Civil War, we put all belligerents in two different "soccer groups", *Pazzesco* and *Mucholoco*. Let's take a look the position of Sheikh Qardhawi at the time of Lebanon – Israel war, 2006:

Pazzesco	*Mucholoco*
Sheikh Nasrallah	**Israel** was against
Lebanese Hezbollah	Syria since the latter
Syria	was helping Hezbollah
	in 2006 war

As the Syrian Civil War erupts, the group is changing; an amazing polarization happens, it is regrouping in 2013 with Syria and Israel still same on their previous position:

Pazzesco	*Mucholoco*
Sheikh Nasrallah	Sheikh Qardhawi
Lebanese Hezbollah	Syrian Rebels
Syria	**Israel**
Supported by Russia	*Supported by USA*

Since Sheikh Qardhawi is not happy with the game result, and then he switches side and entering **Mucholoco** team which warmly welcome him. Meanwhile, Sheikh Nasrallah is not happy either with the game results so he encourages the Lebanese Hezbollah spectators to enter the game field to make the game more interested, meanwhile Lebanese President urges the Lebanese Hezbollah to pull out from Syrian power game. Any result of this game, the spectators are always happy since they are watching an interesting war game, free of charge. Just in case Sheikh Qardhawi or Sheikh Nasrallah is using the religious symbol, the spectators do not necessarily understand since it is a personal opinion and does not represent the scholar majority.

The game is so rude and in some cases is brutal, after 15 minutes the referee issues a yellow card to Nasrallah while the supporters of *Mucholoco* team clapping aloud; but within next 5 minutes the referee issues another yellow card, now for Qardhawi; nobody clapping after exhausting. Anyway, the final winner is the arm producers; the longer the war the better. The arm producers and arm dealers prevail, goaaal!

Since the religious edict or *fatwa* to **wage jihad** against Bashar Assad was issued by Sheikh Qardhawi in Qatar UAE on May 31, 2013 and made public by **Al-Jazeera** TV station; as of June 22, 2013 eleven countries has vowed to "follow his fatwa". Whenever Qardhawi issued a fatwa and the people followed him, *de facto* he is the *Imam* (leader); and the *Ma'moms* (followers) are Britain, France, Germany, Egypt, Italy, Jordan, Qatar, Saudi Arabia, Turkey, United Arab Emirates, and the United States. This *jama'at* (group) is now in one side following Qardhawi the *real deal* leader of eleven countries plus Israel. This *jama'at* is now "*waging jihad*" against Bashar Assad as instructed by their Imam, Sheikh Qardhawi. Meanwhile, on the other side Imam Hassan Nasrallah is leading the *jama'at* of Bashar Assad loyalists, Lebanese Hezbollah, Iranian Shia, and Iraqi Shia. This is an unprecedented *jama'at* and coalition between 12 Moslem and non-Moslem countries; they are now obeying a Moslem Imam face-to-face with other *jama'at* and coalition of Bashar Assad loyalists, Lebanese Hezbollah, Iranian Shia, and Iraqi Shia under the leadership of other Imam, Hassan Nasrallah.

Now, each team of *Pazzesco* with Captain Nasrallah and *Mucholoco* with captain Qardhawi has the different players:

Pazzesco	*Mucholoco*
Sheikh Nasrallah	Sheikh Qardhawi
Iranian Shia	Syrian Rebels
Iraqi Shia	Britain
Lebanese Hezbollah	Egypt
Syria, Bashar loyalists *Supported by Russia*	France
	Germany
	Israel
	Italy
	Jordan
	Qatar
	Saudi Arabia
	Turkey
	United Arab Emirates
	United States of America

This is a bizarre regrouping; and the past history of each player is even more astonishing than their present coalition. Iraq and Iran were in war for 10 years, now they are in the very same *Pazzesco* team. During 2006 Lebanese War, Israel was only supported by USA, now in the fighting against Syria and subsequent Lebanese Hezbollah, Israel was supported by Britain, France, Germany, Egypt, Italy, Qatar, Saudi Arabia, Turkey, United Arab Emirates, and the USA plus Jordan as the relief player, all under Qardhawi the captain of *Mucholoco* team. Qardhawi himself in 2006 was against Israel and on the same side with Lebanese Hezbollah; and he issued fatwa that fighting Israel was a religious obligation. Now, it's a very exciting concept and radical polarization, he is now on the same side and same direction with Israel a country he fought for years! The Syrian Civil War has brought an unprecedented *jama'at* and coalition which never ever happened before. Back to 1967, all Arab countries Egypt, Jordan, Syria, Saudi Arabia, Lebanon, etc. were against Israel; anyway as of June 22, 2013 the geopolitics of Middle East countries has radically and dramatically changed.

When in 1967 Israel itself could overcome the Arab countries, and now with the direct or indirect support of *jama'at* of Moslem countries including Egypt, Jordan, Qatar, Saudi Arabia, Turkey, and United Arab Emirates; Israel will be even easier to overcome Syria, or at least it would be more devastating situation for Syria than ever; this now weak country would be tore off into pieces at the cost of the Syrian civilians especially the women who were suffering from rape and abuse.

Once a war starts, it is not important anymore what the cause that incites it; the main objective is to defeat the adversary; **Sun Tzu**'s doctrine of war is clear, the discipline to overcome the enemy and accomplice is crucial, even if your wife is disobedient she has to be eliminated. This is one among the doctrines of war according to political science. No matter Syria is right or wrong, and no matter Israel is right or wrong; the power talks, if a country is powerful it prevails; Ibn Khaldoun doctrine said "*The history is always written by the winner*"; and who will trust the looser? (Bahry, "*John F. Kennedy's Nuclear War*", 2013; pp. 6-7). The polarization and regrouping among former adversaries in the Middle East plus Europe is now a natural process, **Confucius** has taught us that *an enemy of the enemy is a temporary friend* until a time comes to separate each other.

Syrian Civil War is a political struggle, a struggle for power, and nothing to do with any religion; Shias and Sunnis have been living side by side peacefully for decades without the formation of such *jama'at* and coalition as we witness today. Syrian Civil War is a struggle to hold the power and natural resources; it's a proxy war, it's a competition to grab a bunch of money; therefore the use of religious symbol by both side of Qardhawi and Nasrallah is a misrepresentation. Based on the Hadist # 1392 of "Riyadhus-Salihin" and the Qor'an Chapter 49 verse 9-13; two red cards are presented to Qardhawi and Nasrallah, they are fired.

10. Sarah Palin Phenomenon

Syrian Civil War has entered the most critical stadium, the Moslem kills the fellow Moslem without any sense of shame. The UN has several resolutions concerning Syria while majority of Middle East Moslem countries are against Syria or at least keep silent; they should have been learned from Angelina Jolie who is promoting the peace in Syria, and from Sarah Palin who pronounced "Allah-Akbar" even more persuasive than Nasrallah and Qardhawi.

Former Governor of Alaska Sarah Palin's speech during the annual meeting of **Faith & Freedom Coalition** in Washington, DC June 15, 2013 has drawn the international attention since the analysts perceived it as her surprise move on the political stage. Even though the event she speaks on is not an international political meeting, but the resonance of her speech is politically echoing around the globe especially the Arab and Moslem world since she eloquently pronounced "Allah-Akbar" and "Allah". Here is a passage of her monumental speech "…. *Well, in these radical Islamic countries who aren't even respecting basic human rights, where both sides are slaughtering each other as they scream over an arbitrary red line, 'Allah-Akbar.' I say until we've someone who knows what they're doing, I say, let Allah sort it out.*" (http://www.huffingtonpost.com/2013/06/15/ sarah-palin-syria_n_3447212.html; http://www.washingtontimes.com/news/2013/jun/16/sarah-palin-syria-let-Allah-sort-it-out/; http://abcnews.go.com/blogs/politics/2013/06/sarah-palin-on-u-s-decision-on-syria-let-Allah-sort-it-out/).

Palin's stance on refraining from providing the arm assistance to the Syrian rebels to topple Bashar Assad is a sign of her extraordinary political vision and maneuver agility in a surprising chance to return to political arena. Sarah Palin is even more mature than her former running mate the 2008 Presidential candidate, Senator John McCain, on providing assistance to the Syrian rebels; her political maturity has been far preceding those of McCain. She deserves to be nominated by the Republicans as the next Presidential candidate in 2016 facing the possibility of resurfacing Hillary Clinton.

Whenever, Sarah Palin and Hillary Clinton were nominated for the next presidential candidates, and then the 2016 presidential election would be the victory for all American women; both Republicans and Democrats, no matter either Clinton or Palin would be the winner. Sri Lanka has Sirimavo Bandaranaike as female Prime Minister (and the very first female PM in the world) and female President Chandrika Kumaratunga, India has Indira Gandhi as female Prime Minister, Finland has female President Vigdís Finnbogadóttir, Indonesia has female President Megawati Soekarnoputri; and even the Philippines have two female Presidents **Maria Corazon Sumulong Cojuangco-Aquino** and **Gloria Macapagal-Arroyo.** The USA? Although it is the most advanced democratic country in the world, it has no female President yet, let either Clinton or Palin be the next.

The moves of Palin and Jolie's toward the solution of Syrian conflict peacefully –or least reducing the bloodshed- have embarrassed the Moslem leaders, since the both as the popular international public figures to have more attention than those of Moslem leaders today. As Palin addresses the Syrian conflict where both Moslem groups are chanting "Allah-Akbar" and then slaughter each other which benefiting non-Moslem country; at the same time the Moslem leaders Nasrallah and Qardhawi are cursing each other. Who is more eloquent to pronounce "Allah-Akbar" to address the Syrian Civil War, the Moslem leaders or a Sarah Palin?

11. Egypt (2): Pseudo Patriotic Pride

Arab Spring swept the Arabs away from the truth if they do not follow the **Sunnah**, the legitimate guidance under the Qor'an and Prophet's tradition. It may flip the democratic reform into بطولة "*botoola*" a pseudo patriotic pride which prefers the fight regardless of the reason for it. The "*botoola*" would be always narrated in the tribal gatherings, the descendants of the "hero" would tell the story of the "heroic forefather" in the past. For this reason, the history recorded some conflicts and battles in the Arab world with the vague reasoning.

Want some examples? Sadam Hussein invaded Kuwait just for "*botoola*"; Iraq – Iran War was just for "*botoola*" without ever regarding that the third party may incite the war to drain the oil money from both countries while they were happily fighting for 8 years. In 1979, a group of Moslem extremists put the Mecca Holy Mosque under siege during the pilgrim session in the month of *Dzulhijja*. They declared that the ultimate Imam who would lead all Moslems prior to the end of the world has come, and the Holy Mosque of Mecca should have been "cleaned". The Moslem extremists who declared to follow the *Sunnah* were actually breached it. The *Sunnah* said that the battle during the sacred months (i.e. *Moharram, Rajab, Zolqa'dah* and *Zolhijjah* in the Islamic calendar) is strictly prohibited, and the Moslem extremists did it in 1979 while it was illegal and prohibited without looking into any possibility that the third party was inciting their action.

Now, the world once more time becomes the witness when the "*botoola*" is taking an action to topple Morsi the first freely and democratically elected President of Egypt. Initially, the Tahrir Square movement to topple President Hosni Mubarak was good and on the track of democracy, even when Mohammad Morsi was elected as the next President in the first democratic election it's still good. But, as Morsi applied the Islamic Constitution which was opposed by some groups of Egyptians, and then military *coup d'etat* happens under Abdel Fattah Al-Sisi. General Al-Sisi was even promoted by Morsi to be the Egyptian military commander and now he deposes his promoter; a prophecy has come true that one among the signs of hypocrisy is betrayal over the trust. The Egyptians and any nation have the rights to change the Constitution democratically; however a *coup d'etat* is an official crime against the democratic administration.

The military commanders either in the Moslem or non-Moslem countries, in some occasions took the democratic administration over in *the coup d'etat* just for reason of pseudo "heroism" or "*botoola*" without even considering that their actions were incited by the external power. It is a matter of psychological game rather than power game since the actors were motivated to leave the heroic legacy behind to remember in the future.

With the understanding to this psychological realm inside the military, and then it's uncomplicated for the certain power to encourage the military to stage a *coup d'etat*. The military was always taught to be brave, obedient and upfront of any other citizen; but the democracy never been taught properly. Because the military General has to be brave and then he did a *coup d'etat* and killed the fellow citizen in Chile under General Augusto Pinochet. Because the military General has to be brave and then he did a *coup d'etat* and killed the fellow citizen in Indonesia under General Soeharto. Because the military have to be brave and then they did a *coup d'etat* to cancel the victory of **Front Islamique du Salut** (FIS, Islamic Salvation Front) which democratically won the election, forced President Chadli Benjedid to resign, killed the fellow citizen in Algiers, and sparked the long bloody civil war from 1992 – 2002 and killed around 200,000 fellow Moslems. Because the military General has to be brave and then General Pervez Musharaf did a *coup d'etat* to topple democratically elected Prime Minister Nawaz Sharif in 1999; the end result is Pakistan becomes a field of bloody proxy war where almost every day the civilians were killed in part as the spillover of Afghan War. Because the military have to be brave and then Al-Sisi did a *coup d'etat* to topple Morsi who was freely and democratically elected as Egyptian President. The military commanders who took the democratic administration over in the *coup d'etat* used to be psychologically convinced that they would not prevail over the external power and foreign threat, and therefore they had to show their forces off by destroying the democratic administration as a proof of bravery, while it's not the heroism and bravery, it's the cowardice. When the Algerian military took the administration over in 1992, and then the Middle East despots such as Zein Al-Abedeen of Tunisia, Kaddafi of Libya, and Hosni Mubarak of Egypt immediately supported the *coup* since they were so scared if their powers would be swept away by the grass root movements as Pharaoh kingdom was shattered off into pieces by heroic Israelis grass root movement led by Moses. The history recorded they were all gone; and now some leaders are lauding Al-Sisi *coup* over Morsi administration. *L'histoire répéter?*

The political turmoil in Egypt has a potential of similar misery in Algeria after *coup d'etat* in 1992 which cancelled the democratic victory of Islamic party in the election. Regardless of whether the ideology of Soekarno of Indonesia (http://en.wikipedia.org/wiki/List_of_successful_coups_d%27%C3%A9tat), Isabel de Peron of Argentina, Algerian FIS, Salvador Allende of Chile, Morsi of Egypt, Nawaz Sharif of Pakistan is; all of them democratically won the election. Democracy is the best administration system, but not the most powerful; *Anaídeia* is the most powerful administration system in the world. Anaídeia derived from the Greek "a" or "an" (means "without") and "*aidos*" (means "shame"); Anaideia does mean "*no shame*" or "*shameless*" (*Bahry*, "**John F. Kennedy's Nuclear War**", 2013; p. 1). The old wisdom said "If you have no shame, and then do whatever you want". Morsi might be wrong when he did not share power and talk with the opposing groups in Egypt especially in the very crucial moment between June 30 and July 3, 2013; however Al-Sisi *coup d'etat* has a potential of bloody civil war for 8 years to kill 200,000 fellow Egyptian Moslems as happened in Algeria. It has also a potential of destabilizing the Middle East peace for decades to come. The Middle East countries should have learned on how stable and democratic the USA and Israel are. Israel is a small country compared to Arab countries, yet Israel is most democratic state in the Middle East ever, everything is due process in Israel; the justice system works well in Israel and USA. Israel is the only country in the Middle East which sent its President (Moshe Katsav) to the prison and sentenced lot of its high level government officials after the fair trial; and the USA is the only country in the world which sent its Vice President (Spiro Agnew) to jail. The Middle Eastern countries should have learned from Israel and USA about lot of thing including but not limited to democracy.

Despite the call from Egyptian groups to restore Morsi as Egyptian President, the military defends to detain Morsi; they also criticized the Western countries inconsistency to name Egyptian military action against Morsi as a *coup d'etat*. The Indonesian Human Rights Watch issued a statement in July 2013 that the Egyptian military *coup d'etat* is a serious violation against humanity.

Indonesia has a special sweet memory and relation with Morsi since he was one among Egyptian volunteers during Atjeh tsunami disaster in 2004. Dr. Morsi, a US-educated scholar is a memorizer of the whole Qor'an which consists of 30 parts or 114 chapters; it's a rare expertise even among the Moslem scholars themselves. He still lives in a rented house and has not taken his presidential salary home yet since he was sworn in as Egyptian President. A surprise comes from Sheikh Qardhawi who demands the restoration of Morsi and condemns the *coup d'etat*; Qardhawi has a strong influence in the Middle East, but now who will hear him?

The bloody Egyptian Civil War actually has begun on Sunday night of June 30, 2013 when the mob of Egyptian youths attacked the Islamic Brotherhood Headquarters in Cairo. The youths were provoked that the Islamic Brotherhood "took the power by force" and thus should be ousted by force, and they were also provoked that the Islamic Brotherhood "would kill them". The political theory said that a stone threw by the third party to the one among two opposing parties would surely incite the war between them. This is what happened in Cairo on June 30, 2013; the ensuing bloody conflict (if not a war) would follow automatically; initially "only" 6 people dead on June 30, and then 51 more in July 7, 2013; and then maybe more and more; and maybe spreading across Middle East.

To prevent the situation from being worst, the **Al-Azhar Scholars' Front** after declaring that Dr. Mohamed Morsi is the legal president of Egypt which is freely and democratically elected; and then called for Al-Azhar University and Mosque's Grand Shaikh Ahmed al-Tayyib to leave his post immediately since he offered a false religious cover for the coup against Morsi. The President of **Al-Azhar Scholars' Front** Dr. Yahya Ismail on July 9, 2013 offered a religious preach (khotbah) at the Rabia Adawiyya Mosque of Cairo that the coup against President Morsi is legally forbidden (haram) according to the religious teachings.

Never be in the long history of Al-Azhar since the Fatimid dynasty, a President (Grand Sheikh) of Al-Azhar was publicly criticized and demanded to resign. Al-Azhar is a leading religious school which always considers its every decision on the religious teaching; the demand to a sitting Al-Azhar President to resign is a clue that he was considered as violating Islamic rule, it's a stigma that would tarnish his reputation for good even after his death later.

At last, after first Friday of Ramadan rally, 12th July 2013, the USA seeks the end of Mohammad Morsi detention. However; some critics said that it's a slip of tongue made by state department spokeswoman Jennifer Psaki after being asked about German's Foreign Ministry request to end the restrictions on Dr. Morsi and allow an international organization/the Red Cross to have access to him. Upon a journalist question, it was reported that Jennifer Psaki, who has only very limited option, answered *"We do agree."* According BBC report from Washington, DC July 12, 2013; so far, Washington had avoided publicly calling for the release of Mohammad Morsi, the US only "urging the Egyptian army to stop arbitrary arrests without specifically referring to the deposed president." (http://www.bbc.co.uk/news/world-middle-east-23296463).

Germany is the first Western country to demand the release of Morsi; albeit the Egyptian military is preparing to indict Morsi instead of releasing him from detention. Now, the Egypt Civil War has really begun.

The Egyptians should have remembered Mohammad Abduh when he was lamenting in 1885:

لقدذهبت إلي الغرب ووجدت إسلاما ولا مسلما
فرجعت الي الشرق فوجدت مسلما ولا إسلاما

"(When) I went to the West I saw Islam but no Moslems; then I came back to the East I saw Moslems but not Islam."

Chapter Five: Misunderstood Verses

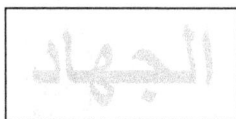

الجهاد

1. Jihad

Jihad is a misunderstood concept. It is an Arabic word, it does have an original meaning of "strive hard or struggle", it is derived from the verb of *"jahada"* or to struggle; the *"holy war"* is not always the perfect translation because the context in every verse containing word of "jihad" is always different. It is true that the main jihad is struggle within a Moslem himself; jihad in any form is not a war against the fellow Moslem.

In the Qor'an there are at least four verses concerning the jihad where the term of *"jihad"* was openly mentioned in different form:

(1) **"Jaahid"** *(please perform jihad)*

> *O Prophet Mohammad; please perform the jihad against the pagans (koffaar) and the hypocrites, and be harsh against them; their abode is the Hellfire, that is the worst destination (9:73). O the believers fight the **koffaar** who are close to you and let them find harshness in you; and you know that God is with the pious people* (**9:123**).

Explanation:

The term of "*Jaahid*" or perform the jihad is used in this verse; it is imperative and obligatory verb. This verse was revealed to Mohammad after the Hodaeboyah Truce in 6 H/628 AD.

The background of the revelation was the existence of a truce between Moslems and the disbelievers; both parties agreed to a 10-year ceasefire, but they generated the chaos by spreading the disinformation and prepared to fight the Moslems. One amongst the disinformation spread by the disbelievers was a fabricated scandal about Prophet Mohammad's relatives. From this perspective of history, we know that Arab knew already the disinformation method in a conflict 1400 years ago.

The next verse i.e. verse 74 of At-Taobah was a warning to Prophet Mohammad about the surrounding people who were very nice in the lips but to have a conspiracy to kill him. The command from God to fight the disbelievers and the hypocrites is an obligation to prepare a real war; while a four-month period were offered for the disbelievers to comply with the truce or to face the war which would be started first by the Moslem. This is the ethics of war as taught by Prophet Mohammad. To start the war is allowed under the special circumstances like the disbelievers who intentionally break up the truce. The war has to be announced prior to its initial attack, this is the Islamic ethic of war and this is the bravery, not cowardice.

If during a grace period of four months the disbelievers to comply with the existing truce and stop the chaos then the war should be cancelled, and in the other hand four months is a reasonable waiting period to skip the sacred months if any.

(2) *"Jaahadoo"* or "they did the jihad"

Indeed, the Messenger and the believers who with him to do jihad along with their wealth and lives in the course of God; the good deeds are for them, and surely they are successful **(9:88).**

Explanation:

The term used in this verse is *"Jaahadoo"* or "they did the jihad", it is a past tense verb indicating the job **was done**.

This verse was telling about the comparison between those who went with Mohammad to the war(s) and those who were sitting down at home after asking the exempt from the war (**9:86**). The verse 88 of Surah At-Taobah was also telling the reward for the warriors both in this world and in the hereafter.

(3) *"Jaahid-hom"*, *do the jihad against them*

So obey not the pagans (kaafirien), and do jihad against them by the Qor'an with ultimate jihad (**25:52**).

Explanation:

In this verse the "jihad" term is mentioned twice, firstly in *"fi'lul-amr"* or obligatory and imperative verb of *"Jaahid-hom"*; and secondly in the *"isim"* or gerund of *"jihadan"*.

Jihad in this verse does mean "tell the truth of Islam to the disbelievers by spreading the Qor'an amongst them". The Qor'an is not a physical weapon and not a tangible tool in a war; therefore this verse should be understood as a command to invite the people into Islam peacefully on the basis of Qor'an teachings (**16:125**). This interpretation is in the domain of '*Tafsier manqool*' or to translate and understand a verse with another verse (see Chapter Four: 3. Tafsier).

"The ultimate jihad" is translated from *"jihaadan kabeera"*, this translation conforms to the decree of Prophet Mohammad when he was asked about the major jihad; upon this inquiry he replied "Jihad against ourselves" (see Chapter Four: 1. Paradigm of Jihad).

(4) *"Jaahid"*, do jihad

O Prophet Mohammad, do jihad against the pagans (koffaar) and the hypocrites, and be austere against them. And their abode is the Hellfire; this is the worst destination (**66:9**).

Explanation:

The term used in this verse is "*Jaahid*" or "do the jihad", it is an obligatory verb for the Moslems to do the jihad as mentioned in the previous commentaries (1) and (3), and it depends upon the context and condition. The war is only the last choice when nothing else available but the fight as done by Prophet Mohammad especially the last war in Tabok, Syria when 300,000 external warriors were invading the Arab peninsula, Prophet Mohammad brought his men **outside** the city to avoid the casualties amongst the civilians.

It is a matter of fact that the Moslems today are weak, poor, uneducated, under the unjust government, in bad health and to kill each other like Iran vs. Iraq (1980 – 1988) or civil war in Syria (2011 – now); so the major jihad *is to increase the quality of Moslem life, eliminate the inconvenience conditions to please God; and not to create the bad condition in any form to make it worst*. The wealthy Moslem countries have the obligation to help their Moslem brothers and sisters in the jeopardy instead of spending the money for fun. What is the rationale of spending some million dollars to rent Disney Land for 60 friends only to celebrate a graduation? How many schools and mosques could be built with 20 million dollars a Moslem spent in May 2013 just for fun?

Now is the era of third wave, Alvin Toffler paradigm of information is a new articulation and "*tafsier*" to Surah Al-Asr; the Moslems should have formulated the perfect meaning of verses and Surahs of Al- Qor'an the way Averroes (Ibn Roshd), Avicenna (Ibn Sina) and Ibn Kathir did to answer the contemporary challenges. The jihad is a continuous effort to invite the mankind into Islam and Qor'an perusal periodicals. The establishment of Islamic schools is much better than building an arsenal and producing the explosives. The building of hospitals and research laboratories for the benefit of Moslems is much profitable than depositing the money in Swiss banks; any time the Moslem depositor died then the money vanished since he never named the beneficiary. The adoption of an orphan is more beneficial than getting married several wives. This is true jihad for this century.

The original meaning of jihad is the effort to obtain something peacefully like an Arabic phrase "*Jaahadtu lin-najaah fid-diraasah*" or I do jihad to obtain my degree. The legitimacy of jihad can be stated briefly: The jihad is not the action of violence against the innocence or unrelated people. The extended meaning of jihad is fighting against the aggressor not to make the aggression. If a jihad -in the meaning of war- is necessary it should be fairly declared, and because the nature of war is the possibility of violence then it should be far away from the unrelated people. The Prophet Mohammad always led the army outside the populated town during his all wars against the disbelievers except one when the Confederate of the disbelievers put the city of Medina under the siege for twenty days. It was one and only war amid the civilians, even in the Conquest of Mecca no single drop of blood was shed. The essence of jihad is to fight the evil distraction within a Moslem; everyone and every group has their own jihad with the different words. Moses and his people did jihad against Pharaoh and against themselves after the covenant of Ten Commandments, Jesus (Isa) and his students group the Hawary did jihad against the hypocrites, and Mohammad and his companions did their own jihad. There are some important verses concerning jihad and the related meanings:

1.1. Fight

1.1.1. *And fight in the course of God those who fight against you, and no transgressing the limit. Truly, God likes no transgressors* (**2:190**).

Explanation:

Term used is "*qaatiloo*", it is the obligatory verb or "*fi'lul-amr*" for the plural; the obligatory verb for single person is "*qaatil*". "*Qaatiloo*" does mean perform the war, while "*uqtuloo*" (**2:191**) does mean kill, an obligatory verb for the plural.

This verse is the first one of the serial verses that has been revealed to Mohammad about "war", "campaign", "fight" and so forth; it has the addendum in another verse such as **9:36**.

This verse is an obligation to fight whenever the attacking polytheists come, no reason for the Moslem to turn his back or to collaborate with the enemy as the hypocrite did in the Confederates and Ohod Wars. If they surrender they should be treated accordingly (**76:8-10**), "**and no transgressing the limit**" means the torture is strictly prohibited even though they are the annoying invaders.

1.1.2. *If they cease, then God the Most Forgiver the Most Merciful (2:192). And fight them until there is no more "fitnah" (bad conditions such as polytheism, chaos, etc.) and until the worship is for God merely; but if they cease then no transgressing but for the "zalimoon" (the wrong doers or those who do the inappropriate deeds)* **(2:193).**

And fight them until there is no more fitnah (polytheism, chaos, uprising etc.) and until the religion will be completely for God; and if they stop from worshipping other than God then certainly God will see what they do **(8:39).**

Explanation:

"And fight them" is translated from "*waqtoloohom*" and "*waqaateloohom*" with the same meaning, this is one of the main objective of war i.e. to restore the order after the chaos. The fight is obligatory against the aggressor, but as they surrender or cease then the fight has to be terminated, and the prisoners of war (POW) have to be treated accordingly with food, and shelter; no torture allowed.

Islam has a specific rule about the POW; Mohammad told the Moslems to take care of them and maintain their rights; God grants the Paradise to the Moslems who take care of the POW (**76:8-10,** and see Ethics of War).

1.1.3. *Then you, Mohammad, should fight in the course of God, you are not assumed responsible but for yourself, and arouse the believers (to fight along with you), may God restrain the evil of the pagans (kafaroo); and God is Stronger in authority and Stronger in punishing* (**4:84**).

Explanation:

Term used is *"fa qaatil"*; it does mean go to the war; it is the obligatory verb or *"fi'lul-amr"*, it is an imperative. This verse was revealed to Mohammad in 626 AD to fight the oncoming enemy avenging on their loss one year before in the Ohod War.

Abu Sofyan the leader of the disbelievers upon his defeat in the Ohod War said to the Moslems that he and his people wanted another war in the village of Badr one year later. When the time came, God urged Prophet Mohammad to intercept the oncoming enemy even by himself **"you are not assumed responsible but for yourself***"* because some companions repudiated a battle since they just did a major war one year before, even some of them were still recovering from the injuries.

Upon this revelation of this verse, Prophet Mohammad with a few loyal companions went to Badr outside of Mecca in the 4th year after migrating to Medina. Meanwhile the famine was going on and Abu Sofyan was scary so he sent his spy Noaem bin Mas'od to spread the disinformation amongst the people about the huge power of disbelievers, it turned to be false.

Prophet Mohammad did not care with the bad news and rumor, he just complied with the command of God to go to Badr even by himself, and as he arrived at Badr no single warrior of disbelievers showed up, did not Abu Sofyan.

1.1.4. *And fight all out against the polytheists as they fight against you all out, and know that God is with those who are pious* (**9:36**)

Explanation:

This verse is an exempt for Moslems to go to war during the sacred months if there is the sudden attack; it is not necessary for the Moslems to wait to respond until the sacred months passed by, otherwise they will be attacked defenselessly. Nevertheless, the nature of prohibition for a war during the sacred month mentioned in **2:217** is still valid, starting the war during the sacred months is strictly forbidden (see Chapter Four: Tafsier)

1.1.5. *They (the hypocrites inside Medina) think that the Confederates have not yet withdrawn, and whenever the Confederates come back, they wish they were in the desert among the Bedouins watching about your conditions (news); and if they by your side they will not fight but a little* **(33:20).**

Explanation:

This verse in **not** a command to fight, but the disclosure about the hypocrites who declined to go to war, they were imagining to be out of town in the desert enjoying the life and talking about the siege instead of breaking it out. They thought that the Confederates have not gone yet, so they keep hiding.

This war occurred in 5th year after migration (The Hijrah) or 627 AD. The Confederates were the tribes of Quraysh, Gatfaan, Salem Family, Asad Family, Morrah Family, Ashja' Family, and Nadher Family. They invaded Medina and put it under siege for twenty days before God sent the heavy rain and tornado to destroy them, the Moslems were physically lost because some prominent companions martyred and there was the non-Moslems mutiny inside the city of Medina, but *de facto* and politically the Moslems won, the powerful Confederates were defeated and they never entered Medina for good.

During the critical situation within wartime, the leader of Qoraedhah tribe, Kaab bin Asad betrayed the Moslems and became an accomplice with Hoyai bin Akhtab the leader of Nadhir tribe.

The Qoraedhah tribe was provoked to cancel the coexistence agreement (see Chapter One: Islam) and to join the Confederates to crush the Moslems from inside the city of Medina. The Qoraedhah tribe was a group of non-believers who were allowed to stay inside the city of Medina together with the Moslem long before the siege; their betrayal was very dangerous and was stunning the Moslems.

Upon this betrayal, Prophet Mohammad sent his two companions Sa'ad bin Moadz the leader of Aus tribe and Sa'ad bin Obadah the leader of Khazraj tribe as the envoy to the Qoraedhah tribe (see Chapter Six: Ethics of War).

1.1.6. *The permit to fight is granted to those who were oppressed, and verily God is powerful to help them (22:39). Those who have been expelled from their homes unfairly just because they said: "God is our Lord"* **(22:40).**

Explanation:

The term used is *"yoqaateloona"* or they are fighting. The unjust eviction and the prohibition of confessing that God is the only Lord are amongst the valid reason to fight. God granted the fight for the oppressed people who suffered from the unjust eviction and religious discrimination.

The complete verse of 22:40 is *"Those who have been expelled from their homes unfairly just because they said: "God is our Lord. If God did not control a group of people from the other then the monasteries, churches, synagogues, and mosques have been torn down while the name of God was recited therein so much. Surely, God will help those who obey Him. Verily, God is The Most Powerful The Most Honorable"* **(22:40).**

The fighting against those who are practicing their religious teachings in the monasteries, churches, synagogues and mosques are unlawful (109:1-6). The fighting against another Moslems with the different school (mazhab) is also prohibited, the *Sunnis* are not allowed to fight the *Shias* and vise versa.

God admitted that His name was periodically recited in the monasteries, churches, synagogues, and mosques therefore He protected them from being razed out by the tyrant. This is a guarantee from God in the Qor'an, is there any similar guarantee in the Bible, Torah and Psalm?

1.2. Killing

1.2.1. *And <u>kill</u> them wherever you find them, and turn them out as they turned you out, and remember that the bad accusation (**fitnah**) is worse than <u>killing</u>. Do not attack them at the Holy Mosque of Mecca (Masjidil-Haram) unless they attack you there first. If they <u>attack</u> you then attack them that is the recompense for the pagans (**kaafirien**) (2:191).*

Explanation:

There are three terms of ***kill, killing,*** and ***attack*** in a single verse; these are the translation of three different words. The first is translated from "*waqtuloohom*", the second is from "*qatl*", and the third (attack is mentioned four times) is from "*tuqaatiloo*", "*yuqaatiloo*", "*qaataloo*", and "*uqtuloo*" they are different kind of words but with the same meaning.

The *Masjidil-Haram* (the Sacred Mosque) in Mecca and *Masjidin-Nabawy* (The Prophet's Mosque) in Medina are sanctuaries, the fight in these two sacred sites any time is strictly prohibited.

This is the one and only verse where the term of attack and the related hard words are mentioned *six times* because the pagans were attacking the city of Medina where one among three sanctuaries found. The disbelievers accumulated the huge power from inside and outside Medina to crush the fledging Moslems community in 627 AD. The inside enemy was The Qoraedhah tribe and the outside enemy was the Confederates (see: Chapter Five: the Confederates War).

The sudden equal response is not for the disbelievers only, but also for the Moslems who make the chaos or attack or uprising during the sacred months. In 1979 there was an uprising in *Masjidil-Haram* of Mecca by some rebellious Moslems, they took over the mosque for a couple weeks during the massive pilgrimage (*Zulhijjah* month); there was the fight, some dead and 64 were captured, all of them were publicly executed, no one got the clemency.

1.2.2. *You kill them not, but God did, and you threw them not but God did. And He might put the believers to the test with the good assessment. Verily, God is The Most Hearer Most-Knower* **(8:17).**

Explanation:

"You kill them" is translated from "*taqtuloohom*". This is not the command to the war; it is the explanation from God about what happened in the Badr War when the Moslems were still so a few but successfully defeated the huge amount of pagans about several times more than the Moslems. God sent the unseen Angel Army to kill the pagans by knocking their backs or throwing them with the stone.

1.2.3. *And when the sacred months passed, then kill the polytheists whenever you find them, and capture them and besiege them and keep them under surveillance. But if they repent and perform the prayer and pay the obligatory charity then leave them free. God is Most Forgiving Most Merciful (9:5). And if anyone of the polytheists seeks your protection then grant him the asylum so he can hear the truth of God's verse and then escort him to the place he can be secure, that is because they are the fool people* **(9:6).**

The term used is "*faqtoloo-hom*" or kill them. This is an order to delay the fight against the polytheist combatants as of the time this verse was revealed on tenth day of month of *Zulhijjah* until tenth day of the month of *Rabeul-akher* because they are the sacred months of Islamic calendar. This verse was revealed because the polytheists in Mecca and the adjacent areas were ready to attack the Moslems.

The verse of 9:6 is a guarantee of safety and security for anyone who seeks the asylum from the Moslems regardless of whether he is embracing Islam or not; the main idea is the disbeliever will soon hear the truth of God's verse.

1.3. The War (qitaal)

The third word which is used in correlation with the pagans is "*qitaal*", it does mean war.

1.3.1. *The war has been ordained for you even though you dislike it, and maybe you dislike something but it is good for you, and maybe you like something but it is bad for you. God knows while you do not* (**2:216**).

Explanation:

Term used is "*qitaal*" or the war. The war is painful and something to hate, but if the pagans and enemy combatants have come then the war is obligatory; it happened in 627 AD when at least 7 major Arab tribes established the confederation to destroy the fledging Moslem society in Medina. If the Moslems were defeated in that time then the history is unlike what now we are looking at.

1.3.2. *They were asking you Mohammad concerning the sacred months (i.e. the first, seventh, eleventh, and twelfth months of the Islamic calendar) where the war is in. Say "The war is a great transgression, but a greater transgression with God is to prevent mankind from following the way of God, to disbelieve in Him, to prevent access to the Holy Mosque of Mecca and to evict its residents. And the bad accusation (fitnah) is worse than the killing. And they always fight against you until they turn you back from your religion of Islam, if they can. And whosoever between you turning back from his religion and dies while he/she is a disbeliever (kaafir, atheist or polytheist), then his/her good deeds were annulled both in this world and in the hereafter, they will be the dwellers of Hellfire; they will abide therein forever* (**2:217**).

Explanation:

Term used is "*qitaal*" or the war; it is the "isim" (noun) derived from the verb of "*qaatala*" or to go to war. Some scholars say that this verse is abrogated by verse 36 of *Surah At-Taobah*.

The other scholar consider that both verses are valid and no abrogation because the verse 2:217 explains the prohibition of war during the sacred months while verse 9:36 is a permit to a war during the sacred months if the Moslems are attacked first. Therefore, the nature of war prohibition mentioned in 2:217 is still valid (see Chapter Four: Tafsier).

1.3.3. *O Prophet Mohammad, urge the believers to the war. If there are twenty steadfast persons amongst you, they will be defeating two hundreds enemies, and if there are one hundred steadfast persons they will be defeating one thousand pagans (kafaroo) because they are fool people* **(8:65).**

Explanation:

Term used is "*qitaal*" and translated into war, it is the "*isim*" a noun or gerund derived from verb of "*qatala*".

This is the command for Prophet Mohammad to urge his people to the war in the course of God. During the 'Jaheleyyah' period the war was only a tradition to gain the honor and power to control the resources in a certain land; that was the pagans did and therefore in the end of this verse God explained the different motivation between Moslems and pagans.

This verse was revealed around the Badr War I when the powerful pagans attacked the Moslem society in Medina while they were still so few. God granted to every Moslem the power equal to ten disbelievers when they met in Badr village outside Medina.

1.4. The Weapons

The fourth word which is used in correlation with the pagans is "weapons".

When you Mohammad, are among your companions and to lead them for prayer, then let a part of them to stand up with you while they are bearing their weapons. When they are done with their prostration then let them take the position in the rear line (facing the enemy); and let the other group who have not prayed to come up to do the prayer with you. Please be advised for them to be cautious and to bear the weapons because the disbelievers (kafaroo) so eager to attack you in a "blitzkrieg" as you are negligent of your arms and stuffs. There is no problem with you when you put down your weapons due to inconvenience of rain or sickness as you take every precaution as well. Verily, God has been preparing a humiliating torment for the disbelievers (kaafirien) **(4:102).**

Explanation:

No single term of war used in this verse, but it is a highest alert for Prophet Mohammad about the sudden attack (*blitzkrieg*) from the pagans. The combat readiness during the wartime is obligatory even within the prayer; the Moslems should maintain their obligation to pray five times a day any time even during the war.

How to maintain the balance between the highest alert and the prayer is an art, Prophet Mohammad provided the smart example to his companions.

1.5. The Spoils of War

The fifth word which is used in correlation with the pagans is "spoils of war".

They ask you Mohammad about the spoils of war. Say "The spoils of war are for God and the Messenger". So fear of God and settle the disputes amongst you, and obey God and His Messenger if you are the true believers **(8:1).**

Explanation:

No single direct term of war used in this verse, there is a term of "*anfaal*" (the spoils of war) as a logic consequence of the war. The spoil of war is not the objective of the war, but if it exists such as weapons, vehicles and personal properties they should be managed accordingly to avoid the unfairness between the army.

1.6. The Day of Criterion

The sixth word which is used in correlation with the pagans is "the day of criterion".

And for your information that the war-booty you may obtain, one-fifth of it should be assigned to God, the Messenger, the close relative of Messenger, the orphans, the poor, and the wayfarer when you believe in God and the verse We revealed to Our Messenger on the Day of Criterion the Day of Two Forces met **(8:41).**

Explanation:

No term of war or fight, but there is "*yaomal-talqal jam'aan*" or the day where two forces met; that was the Major Badr War on Ramadan 17, 624 AD a first major war in the second year after Prophet Mohammad's migration from Mecca to Medina.

The Badr War was also named the Day of Criterion, because the on that day the difference between idolatry and faith was obvious and the difference between a disbeliever and a Moslem was clear. The disbelievers who defended the idolatry were in one side and the Moslems who believed in God were in another.

Wayfarer in this verse is translated from "*ibnus-sabeel*", it does mean "the son of road", some scholars translated it as wayfarer, and some of them translated as a Moslem who is traveling from a state to another and has not enough money. He/she deserves the help from the Treasury Board (*Baytul-maal*) that regulates the saving account for the Moslem community.

1.7. Captive

The seventh word which is used in correlation with the pagans is "captive".

O Prophet Mohammad, say to the captives who are in the custody: "If God knows any kindness in your hearts then He will grant you something better than that has been taken from you; and He will forgive you, and God is the Most Forgiver Most Merciful (8:70). But if they intend to betray you, they indeed betrayed God in advance; so He granted you the power over them, and God is The Most Knower Most Wise **(8:71).**

Explanation:

There is no single word of fight or the war, but the captive is related to a war. This verse was telling the Moslem how to treat the captives or the prisoner of war. It is a good idea to compare with the Geneva Convention (see Chapter Six: The Ethics of War).

The objective of war is not to kill the enemy or to revenge but to restore the order, this is the main doctrine of war in Islam. If the main objective of war is to kill the enemy as much as possible then this verse will not tell about the treatment of the captive and Prophet Mohammad will kill all Mecca disbelievers in the day of the Conquest of Mecca.

1.8. Bara'ah, release

The eighth word which is used in correlation with the pagans is "releases".

This is God and His Messenger's declaration of the freedom from obligations to those of the polytheists, with whom you made a treaty (9:1). So you the polytheists can travel freely for four months throughout the land (to prepare the war), but for your information that you cannot defeat God; and God will disgrace the disbelievers (kaafirien) (9:2).

And this is the declaration from God and His Messenger to the mankind on the day of greatest pilgrimage that God and His Messenger are free from all obligations to the polytheists. So if you the polytheists want to repent, that is better for you but if you turn away, then see you cannot escape from the punishment of God. Mohammad; give the warning of a very painful torment to the disbelievers (kafaroo) **(9:3)**.

Explanation:

The Bara'ah is a cancellation of a treaty due to a lawful reason, in 630 AD there was a truce between the Moslems and the disbelievers; the contents of truce among other things are: cease-fire and the Moslems were allowed to visit Mecca from Medina for the pilgrimage.

When *Banu Nadhir* a chaotic tribe in Medina established a new alliance with the other tribes in Mecca and Medina and spread the disinformation to prepare the massive war to retaliate their eviction from Medina in 626 AD then God in 631 AD ordered Mohammad to cancel the existing truce because it was worthless.

This is one and only Surah in the Qor'an started without "*Bismillaahirrahmaanirrahiim*" or 'By the name of God the Most Gracious Most Merciful' at the beginning of its verse, all Surahs (chapters) but this one always started with "*Bismillaahirrahmaanirrahiim*" because this Surah was a declaration of war against the chaotic disbelievers who have had a truce but were preparing a war. Nevertheless, they were granted a four-month grace period to prepare the war they wanted. This is one amongst the ethics of war in Islam; the grace period is necessary as the final choice between complying with the truce or the war.

In the other verse the reason of truce cancellation is explained: "*How come there is such a covenant with them whenever they get a chance they regard no more kinship nor covenant with you. They are so good with their lips to please you but their hearts are averse to you; and most of them are disobedient and rebellious (faasiqoon)*" **(9:8)**.

2. Marriage

The marriage in Islam should be fulfilling some requirements, among other things are the existence of bride and groom, both bride and groom are in the lawful condition to marry, the same gender marriage and incest marriage are unlawful, the guardian or parent to permit, and the pledge for marriage.

The mother, daughter, sister, aunt, niece, the mother-in-breast feeding (she is not a biological mother but gives a breast feeding), the sister-in-breast feeding (she is not a biological sister but receives the same breast feeding from the same lady), mother-in-law, step daughter, daughter-in-law, sister's wife, and the still-in-wedlock lady are subject to unlawful marriage (**4:23-24**).

According to the Islamic law, both bride and groom have to be Moslem during the marriage, if one of them or both of them are not Moslem they should confess "*shahadah*" first, otherwise the marriage is void and the intimate relation would be considered as forbidden adultery.

There are some scholars who allowed inter-faith marriage such as the bride is Moslem and the groom in non-Moslem, or vise versa. They based their opinion on the verse 5 of Surah Al-Ma'edah "*Today I make the good things lawful for you. The foods made from the slaughtered cattle prepared by People of the Holy Scripture are lawful for you and your foods are lawful for them. The chaste women amongst the believers and the chaste women amongst People of the Holy Scripture –who came before you- are lawful for you to marry whenever you have submitted the mandatory dowry to them desiring chastity within the legal wedlock not committing illegal intercourse nor taking them as the girl-friends without marriage (5:5)*".

This case is open for discussion, but the majority of scholar concluded that the inter-faith marriage is void. Their conclusion is based on at least three facts:

(1) Mohammad and other companions never did the inter-faith marriage.

(2) The inter-faith marriage is forbidden according to verse 221 of Surah Al-Baqarah "*And do not ever married the idolaters -who believe in the existence of god other than God the One- until they become the believers in the oneness of God. Indeed, a slave who believes in God is better than an idolater even though she astonishes you. And never permit your daughters to marry the idolaters until they become the believers; verily a believing slave is better than an idolater even he astonishes you because they are inviting you to the Hellfire while God invites you to the Paradise and His Forgiveness by His Grace. God explains His verses to the mankind so they might remember*".

(3) The polytheists are *najs* *) they did not know the way of *istinja* *), they ate the najs and *haram* foods *) such as ham, dog meat **) etc. "*O the believers, verily the polytheists are najs; so let them stay away from the Holy Mosque of Mecca (Masjidil-Haram) after this year. If you fear the poverty, God will make you rich with His bounty if He will, surely God the Most Know the Most Wise*" **(9:28).**

---

*)   *Najs* means filth and impure, **istinja** is the way to clean the body and cloth from filth and body fluid excretion, and *haram* means unlawful, see the Terminology

**) In some remote areas the certain tribe considered the dog meat as a special menu, it sounds uncivilized but that is a fact

Who are People of the Holy Scripture, and who are the idolaters? Back to six fundamental faiths or "Arkaanul- Iman": (1) to believe in one God, (2) to believe in the Angels, (3) to believe in the Holy Scriptures i.e. Abraham's manuscript, Psalm, Torah and Bible or Injeel, (4) to believe in all 25 Messengers, (5) to believe in the Day of Judgment, and (6) to believe in the good and bad fate coming from God. Do People of the Holy Scripture believe in all 25 Messengers including Mohammad, Jesus (Isa) and Moses? The answer is very critical, if they did and believe in all six fundamental faiths (**2:62**) then they are eligible to marry the Moslem, otherwise they have no sufficient requirement.

There was a classic dispute about who are People of the Holy Scripture, who are they?

3. People of the Holy Scripture

To understand the proper meanings of Qor'an verses, a Moslem should learn a various sciences as Tafsier, hadith, Arabic (grammatical, style, etc.), *mustalah hadith*, Asbaabun-Nozool (the context of revelation), *Fiqh* and *Osol-fiqh*, and so on. The understanding to the meaning of People of the Holy Scripture is complicated, even to know who is an idolater is easier. The general meaning of idolater is everyone who does not believe in the existence of God (atheist), or to believe in the existence of the god other than One God i.e. God, or the worshipper of the nature such as sun, moon, star, river, mount etc. is considered as an idolater (**6:75-82**). The people who believe in some gods are also idolaters.

The religions conveyed by the Messengers of God including Moses, Jesus (Isa) and Mohammad are divine. The understanding of People of the Holy Scripture should be traced from the era of Abraham the Father of All Believers. It is a matter of fact that Moses came after Abraham, Jesus (Isa) came after Moses, and Mohammad came after Jesus (Isa); each of them conveyed the divine teaching for the mankind and each of them acknowledged the previous prophet and replaced the previous divine teaching as well.

During Abraham era the existing law was in the Scripture of Abraham, during David era the existing law was in the Psalm, during Moses era the existing law was in the Torah, during Jesus (Isa) era the existing law was in the Bible. And during Mohammad era the existing law is in the Qor'an and it lasts until the Day of Judgment because will be no more prophet after him.

This case is open for discussion, but the majority of scholar concluded that People of the Scripture are not available anymore today. Their conclusion is based on at least three facts:

(1) People of the Holy Scripture are those who believe in the Bible, Torah and Psalm and believe in the next prophecy. Bohaera was an example; he was a famous People of the Holy Scripture who disclosed the signs of Mohammad's prophecy when he met Mohammad during his trip to Syria with Abu Taleb in 583 AD. Bohaera was a scholar who recited the Bible, Torah and Psalm and understood them well where the signs of the last prophet was clearly written such as *"And there came fear on all, and they glorified God saying: That a great Prophet is risen up amongst us"* (**Luke 7:16**).

Some scholars said that the meaning of "A great prophet" is Mohammad because during the lifetime of Jesus (Isa) a prophet had been risen up, therefore "is risen" should be understood as "will be risen"; and "amongst us" does mean amongst the descendant of Abraham. Mohammad son of Abdullah, Jesus son of Mary, John son of Zachary, and Moses were the direct descendants of Abraham.

The other prophecy is **"Nevertheless, I must walk today, tomorrow, and the day following, for it cannot be that a prophet perish out of Jerusalem"** (Luke 13:33). The meaning of *"cannot be that a prophet perished out of Jerusalem"* is after the death of Jesus (Isa) there will be another prophet to visit Jerusalem. During the Night of Journey Mohammad visited Jerusalem in 621 AD together with Gabriel the Angel before ascending to heaven to receive the command of prayer directly from God.

People of the Holy Scripture also believe in the next Messenger mentioned in the Bible as "Comforter": **"If you love me, keep my commandments. And I shall pray to the Lord and He will give you** *another* **Comforter that may abide with you forever"** (John 14:15-16).

(2) The most people who believe in the Bible, Torah and Psalm today do not believe in Mohammad the last Messenger of God.

(3) If someone does not believe in Mohammad the last Messenger then according to the Islamic law he/she is not a believer, if he/she is not a believer he/she cannot marry a Moslem. Nevertheless, beyond the term of marriage; the People of the Holy Scripture still reserve the rights to practice their religious teachings (**109:1-6**); any interference by the Moslem will be considered as a serious violation.

4. Zabeha

Zabeha is the meat of cattle slaughtered under the Islamic law. The eligible cattle for Moslem consumptions are chicken, sheep, goat, cow, and camel; during the slaughter the name of God *"Bismillaahirrahmaanirraahiim"* has to be recited otherwise their meats are unlawful to consume. *"The dead cattle, blood, pig, and every cattle slaughtered without reciting God's name on it, strangled cattle, killed cattle by a violent blow, killed cattle by headlong fall, killed cattle by goring of horn, and killed cattle by wild animal unless you have the chance to slaughter before its death and sacrificed cattle in the cause of idol are forbidden to you to consume as well as using arrow to seek the lucky draw; all of them are the expression of disobedience to God"* (**5:3**). The bloods even from the eligible cattle are unlawful (**2:173, 5:3**) while all kinds of fish are lawful and not necessary to slaughter.

Now, the question is 'what if the lawful cattle like the lamb or cow slaughtered by non-Moslem people, are their meats 'halal' or lawful for Moslems to consume?' The answer is definitive "No", because People of the Holy Scripture are not available anymore today.

This case is open for discussion, but not to dispute over the divine law or to seek the exempt to consume unlawful meats. The conclusion is based on at least two facts:

(1) The most people who believe in the Bible, Torah and Psalm today do not believe in Mohammad the last Messenger of God.

(2) If someone does not believe in Mohammad the last Messenger, then he/she is not a Moslem and not People of the Holy Scripture, if she/or he is not a Moslem or People of the Holy Scripture then he/she cannot slaughter the cattle for the Moslems to consume. If they believe in Mohammad then their food of slaughtered cattle is lawful for the Moslem (4:150-151). This rationale is a method of *istinbaa*t.

Every meat product processed from the eligible cattle but during the slaughter or processing without reciting God's name is unlawful for the Moslems to consume. Therefore any cattle meat available in the common supermarkets throughout the USA, Canada, UK, Europe and other places without legal "*halal*" label is unlawful for the Moslem to consume. This is Islamic law; the Moslems are not necessary to dispute over this divine law or to seek the exempt to consume unlawful meats unless for emergency only. The supermarkets have the rights to sell it but the Moslems are not allowed to consume it.

The Jews never disputed about the 'kosher' law, they maintained the separate containers, spoons and utensils for the specific use; they never used the same utensil for milk and meat even though in the stomach the both will be mixed up. There is a Jewish company to sell the 'halal' meat for the Moslems; the owner hired some Moslems who familiar with the Islamic law. He never intervened in the food processing because he knew what to do; it is a very good example a Jew respects the zabeha Islamic law so why the Moslems are not respecting the Islamic law in preparing the food and seeking the exempt to eat the unlawful meats?

We knew that the common things like marriage, People of The Holy Scripture and Zabeha are actually the subject to dispute with so many opinions and references, so how about the critical subject like Jihad?

Chapter Six: The Doctrine of War

STOP

And prepare for your enemy every power you deserve including steed of war (cavalry and another weapons) to deter the enemy of God and yours and the other parties besides them you do not know right now but God does. Whatsoever you spend in the cause of God it would be reimbursed to you and you will be never cheated" (8:60)

This is the doctrine of war during the lifetime of Mohammad, and under the divine guidance he led his people to go through the hard years of persecution, abuse, betrayal, battle and war during more than 22 years in Mecca and Medina.

There were more than eight minor and major wars under the direct command of Mohammad the Prophet; all of them are **self defense** and nothing of them was an invading war, the first one in 2 H or 624 AD and the last one in 9 H/631 AD for seven years only but with the effect around the world until now in 21st century and the beyond. Nothing compares in the history a commander leads eight wars more within seven years and survives.

We will find out why and when the war occurred during the lifetime of Mohammad, and we will discuss the consequence of war including the truce, status of POW and ethics of war in the Islamic Law.

For more understanding to the doctrine of war in Islam, we are going to briefly highlight the minor and major wars during the lifetime of Mohammad the Prophet, they were Major Badr War, Ohod War, Trench War, Mo'tah War, Minor Badr War, The Conquest of Mecca, Honaen War, and Tabok War.

1. Major Badr War

Thirteen years Prophet Mohammad and his companions were practicing Islam in is their native land amid the harassment of the disbelievers of Mecca. The hate crime forced Mohammad and his companions to leave Mecca for Medina in 622 H. They left their stuffs behind, and the Meccan collected and distributed them as the confiscation for the disbelievers.

The Moslems had been trying to build a new peaceful society far away from Mecca, but the Meccan still so eager to kill Mohammad after their failure to kill him in a chasing from Mecca to Medina in 622 AD. The Mecca pagans have tried with every power to drive Prophet Mohammad out and to kill him just because one reason: he said no god but Allah. Therefore God revealed Mohammad to prepare the militia just in case if the war breaks out:

"The permit to fight is granted to those who were oppressed, and verily God is powerful to help them (22:39). Those who have been expelled from their homes unfairly just because they said: 'God is our Lord'. If God did not control a group of people from the other then the monasteries, churches, synagogues, and mosques have been torn down while the name of God was recited therein so much. Surely, God will help those who obey Him. Verily, God is The Most Powerful The Most Honorable" **(22:40).**

This is the very first verse about preparation of the war, and the main reason is *"Those who have been expelled from their homes unfairly just because they said: 'God is our Lord'"*. Upon this revelation, Mohammad organized the militia to guard inside and outside Medina.

When the Meccan heard that the Moslems found a new basis for practicing the faith then they planned to destroy them. On Ramadan 17, 2 H/624 AD the joint forces of Mecca tribes left for Medina to destroy the Moslems' new peaceful society. Before arriving at Medina they were intercepted at the village of Badr south of Medina and the war was inevitable, later this war was named the Badr Kubra or Major Badr War.

The Moslems were small and weak they were only 313 volunteers but they defeated the joint forces of major Mecca tribes with around 2,000 warriors; and for this significant victory beside the weakness of Moslem, God revealed some verses of Surah Ali Imran:

"And God helped you to the victory at Badr when you were weak, so fear God that you may be thankful (3:123). Remember the day when you Mohammad said to the believers: 'Is it not enough for you that your Lord provides you with three thousand angels which have been sent down?' (3:124). Certainly it is. If you are going to be patience and pious and the enemy comes rushing at you; surely your Lord helps you with five thousand angels having their own mark (3:125). God made it as the glad tidings and as the assurance to your hearts. And there was no victory but from God the Almighty the Wise (3:126). That He might destroy a part of them or expose them to infamy so they returned empty handed and frustrated (3:127). There was nothing of your interference in their case whether God grants the clemency or punishment to them because they were defiant" **(3:128).**

Prophet Mohammad was very sad to know his loyal companions martyred but he was also sad to hear that the leaders of 70 Mecca tribe were killed in the war, he knew a few of them during his lifetime in Mecca. Certainly, Mohammad still reserved a hope that someday they will come back to their tribes to convey the faith and not to die without faith. The world knew how Mohammad went to war without any hatred; he did just for complying with the command of God. The verse 128 of Surah Ali Imran was an explanation to Prophet Mohammad that he could not choose who to die, and God reserved all decisions to which He will grant the mercy or punishment.

This is the famous and decisive war, if Prophet Mohammad was defeated then the history will be different, this war was also named the Day of Criterion (**8:41**) where the difference between idolatry and faith was obvious and the difference between a pagan and a Moslem was clear. The pagans defended the idolatry were in one side and the Moslems believed in God were in another.

2. Ohod War

The defeat of Badr War brought a hammering effect to the coalition of Mecca tribes; they could not understand on why the amount of less than 500 Moslems might defeat them with around 2000 powerful warriors. The victory has to be obtained and the embarrassing defeat should be retaliated, therefore the Mecca disbelievers prepared more than 3000 warriors even with two fresh joining tribes Kinanah and Tihamah. They were positive to be able to destroy the defensive Moslems inside the city of Medina.

On the month of Shaban 3 H/625 AD the Mecca warriors left for Medina. As Mohammad heard the movement of the huge Mecca warriors he led his people outside the city to confront the invaders. Two opposing groups of warrior met in the Valley of Mount Ohod in the middle of Shaban month. Unfortunately, in this critical situation a group of Moslem warriors around 250 led by Abdullah bin Obay dismissed themselves and came back to Medina without participating to the war.

The situation got worst when Salama Family of Aus tribe and Harisah Family of Khazraj tribe asked the exempt from Prophet Mohammad not to participate in the war (**3:122**). Now what to do, the Moslems remain about 700 and the Mecca warriors are 3000 or more? The power was unbalance and the Moslems were initially defeated before regaining the victory. In this war even Prophet Mohammad himself was wounded but not a life-threatening injury.

This injury has generated a very dangerous rumor that Mohammad died in the war; and the rumor has put some Moslems in doubt, even some of them considered to seek refuge from Abu Sofyan the enemy commander. God condemned them in verse 144 of Surah Ali Imran: *"Mohammad is only the Messenger, and some messengers have passed away before him. If he dies or is killed will you turn your backs* (as the disbelievers)?"

In this war Prophet Mohammad as a commander instructed the archery division to stay on a strategic position in any situation until the next order came, but this division left the position because they thought the war was over (**3:152**). During first hour after the archery division left their strategic position, a dozen of Moslems martyred and a prominent companion *Anas bin Nadr* also martyred (see Chapter Six: Suicide Bombing). Most of them then turned their backs and scattered to any place to get the shelter, so when Prophet Mohammad called them nobody responded (**3:153**).

God strongly condemned the betrayal of Abdullah bin Obay and his men; God recalled the betrayal of the hypocrites in Surah of Hypocrites. This Surah also correlates with the betrayal of Qoraedhah tribe of Medina during the Confederates War:

In the name of God the Most Gracious the Most Merciful, When the hypocrites come to you they say: 'We bear witness that you are the real Messenger of God but God bears witness that the hypocrites are liars indeed (63:1). They made their oaths as a shield to conceal the hypocrisy so they might obstruct the people from the path of God. Verily, evil is what they used to do (63:2)."

"That is because they believed and then disbelieve, therefore their hearts are sealed, so they never understand (63:3). And whenever you look at them their body impressed you, and when they speak you listen to their words; but they are like the propped-up woods, and they think that every shout is against them. May God curse them, how come they deviating from the right path (**63:4**)?

3. The Minor Badr War

The pagans' initial victory in the Ohod War in 625 AD was only temporary, when God sent the heavy rain then the war was over, and a year later they were so eager to get revenge, they were so upset because Mohammad did not die. Abu Sofyan said to the Moslems that he and his people wanted another war in Badr one year later; this challenge was accepted by the Moslems and in the next year they went to Badr. When the time came, God urged Mohammad to intercept the oncoming enemy even by himself if his companions were reluctant to go to fight. Some companions repudiated the battle because they just did a year before at the Valley of Mount Ohod. Therefore God revealed this strict verse to Prophet Mohammad: *"Then you Mohammad; should fight in the course of God, you are not assumed responsible but for yourself. And arouse the believers to fight along with you, may God restrain the evil of the pagans (kafaroo); and God is The Stronger in authority and The Stronger in punishing* (**4:84**).

Upon this revelation of this verse, Mohammad with a few loyal companions went to Badr outside of Mecca in 4H/626 AD. Abu Sofyan instead of the retaliation over his downfall, he sent a spy *Noaem bin Mas'od* to propagate the disinformation *) amongst the people about the existence of a huge power of disbelievers. Prophet Mohammad did not care about the bad news he just complied with the command of God to go to Badr even by himself, but as he arrived at Badr no single warrior of disbelievers showed up, did not Abu Sofyan.

Later, God recalled this incident in Surah Ali Imran *"They are the believers to whom the hypocrites say: 'Verily be careful, the men have gathered to fight against you and therefore fear of them'. Anyway, this warning even increased their courage and faiths and they said: 'God is The Sustainer for us, He is The Best Provider'"* (**3:173**).

The news of Badr war made the residents scary and only some merchants went to Badr market on the next day. Since the business was too slow the commodity price was very low, Prophet Mohammad and his companions who were still in Badr bought almost all commodities available at the market and sold them in the Medina market with the significant profit. This incident was narrated by God in Surah Ali Imran: "*They returned with God's Grace and Bounty no a single harm touched them, and they followed the bliss of God. God is the owner of great bounty*" **(3:174).**

This war was named the *Badr Sughra* or Minor Badr War because no fight or resistance from the pagans.

---

*) The ancient Arabs in 626 AD have recognized the art of disinformation; this method has been used as a part of psychological warfare for the superiority of real war.

4. The Confederates War

The attempt to murder Prophet Mohammad never stopped, even when he has settled in Medina the Nadhir tribe tried to murder him, it was another attempt after the failure of Meccan to kill him when he was hiding in *Tsur* cave with Abu Bakr (see Chapter One: Islam). To ensure the assassination of Mohammad and to destroy the Moslem society in Medina, so many tribes united to establish the Confederates. The enemy was completely surrounding the Moslems from inside and outside Medina. The inside enemy came from Medina residents of Nadhir and Qoraedhah tribes; and the outside one came from Mecca pagans united in the Confederates.

The Confederates successfully accumulated more than 10,000 warriors to invade Medina in 5 H/627 AD; it was a biggest amount ever since. Almost all Meccan tribes such as Quraysh, Gatfaan, Salem, Asad, Morrah, and Ashja' and even the Nadher and Qoraedhah tribes of Medina united in an attempt to crush the Moslems settled in Medina. They put Medina under siege for **twenty seven** days before God sent the heavy rain and tornado to destroy them. The Moslems were physically lost and some prominent companions like *Saad bin Moadz* martyred; there was the non-Moslems mutiny inside the city of Medina, but *de facto* and politically the Moslems won. The powerful Confederates were defeated and they never entered Medina. In our modern age now, we could never understand what happened if our city of 3,000 residents is under siege for 27 days while more than 10,000 troops surrounding us.

The prolonged siege has made the Quraysh army impatient since they could not proceed into the city of Medina nor the Moslems inside the city came out. In this situation, a strongest and bravest among the Quraysh army named **Amr bin Abdul-Wudd** challenged any Moslem for duel. To respond this challenge, Mohammad the Prophet sent his cousin **Ali bin Abi Taleb** to accept the duel challenge. The duel was so intense to stir the dense dust covering the two fighting heroes. Both the fighters were totally lost inside the swirling desert dust and nobody knew what was happening until the both sides hear the loud screams indicating a painful blow. The tension was covering both sides and everybody was so curious about who's screaming, was he Ali or Amr. Anyway, when a chanting of "Allah Akbar" (God the Greatest) coming from the whisk of dust, the both side knew that Ali prevailed since Amr would never say this divine chanting. The death of Amr bin Abdul-Wudd discouraged the confederates and they decided to withdraw from besieging Medina in a state of panic and disarray.

Two famous Confederates generals Amr bin Ass As-Sahmy and Khalid bin Waled Al-Makhzoomy retreated to Mecca and later they embraced Islam after realizing that the huge power of more than 10,000 warriors they commanded could not defeat a couple thousand Moslem people defended Medina. Even later on, after his conversion to Islam *Khalid bin Waled* led the Moslem militias in the Mo'tah War against the Romans in 630 AD.

This war was named the *Ahzaab* or Confederates War because the disbelievers united in a confederation, and it was also named the Trench War because the city of Medina surrounded by the artificial trenches invented by *Salman Al-Farisy* a Persian companion. The trenches were dug north side of Medina to prevent the enemy from entering the city, and this was the first time the trench was used in a war as the defense system. This is the one and only war during Mohammad occurred around the populated city, Mohammad used to lead the Moslem warrior outside the city to avoid the casualties amongst the civilians.

The Trench War was the massive defense against the united invaders and was the hardest one ever since, the Moslems condition in that time was so bad after another war i.e. the Ohod War where 70 prominent companions **martyred**, even though the Moslems were able to defeat the Confederates. Their loyalty and combat readiness appreciated much by God with His verse in Surah Ali Imran: *"They still obeyed God and His Messenger (in the Trench War) even after being wounded (in the Ohod War). Definitely, the great recompense was awarded to those amongst the Moslems who did the good achievement and feared God"* **(3:172).**

God also recalled this famous war in Surah of The Confederates with a long verse: "*O the believers, remember the blessing of God to you when The Confederates invaded you, then We sent the tornado and the invisible and invincible army. God is The Most Watcher to what you did (33:9). When they came to you from every direction and when the eyes were upside down because of fear and when the breath was scarcely reaching the throat and when you were in doubt about the oncoming help from God (33:10). There, the believers were tested and they were quaked with a sudden shock (33:11). When the hypocrites and those who have the illness of doubt in their hearts said: 'The promise of God and Mohammad is nothing but a delusion to us' (33:12). And when a group of people said: 'O the people of Yasreb, there were no stand for you against the attack, so go back!' And suddenly a group of Moslems asked for the exempt from the Prophet pretending of 'Excuse me, I'll go back because no guard at home' while in fact their homes are open safely; they want nothing but evading the war* (33:13)."*

"And whenever the city of Medina is under the heavy attack from every track and the residents are asked to renegade from Islam to polytheism then they definitely do it right away and will never cancel it but for a while (33:14). In fact, they already made a covenant with God that they never ever be traitors. Indeed, such a covenant will be accountable for (33:15). Mohammad, say to them: 'The escape is not beneficial to you if run away from the death or from the war, if you do you will not enjoy but a while (33:16). Mohammad, say to them: 'Who can protect you from God if He determines to harm you or to bless you?' Surely, they never found any custodian or guardian but God (33:17). Amongst you, God knew exactly who did hold you back from fighting in the cause of God and He knows who do say to their relatives: 'Come on, go with us' while they do not go to the battle but to play around (33:18). They despaired to you, when the fear comes; you see them looking at you with upside down eyes like unconscious person encountering a death but, when the fear disappears they smite you with the sharp tongues while they are tightfisted to do the good deeds. They are disbelievers (lam yo'minoo) and God makes their previous good deeds void; that is easy for God (33:19). They think that the Confederates have not yet withdrawn, and whenever the Confederates come back, they wish they are in the desert among the Bedouins watching your conditions; and if they by your side they will not fight but a little (33:20").

"In fact, there is an excellent example in the personality of Mohammad for those who expects to meet God and to be comfortable in the Day of Judgment and for those who always remember God (33:21). And when the believers saw the Confederates they said: 'This is what God and His Messenger had promised us, God and His Messenger said the truth'. And they became more faith and submissive to God (33:22). Amongst the believers there are the men, who maintain their covenant to God, and some of them fulfilled the obligation as martyr, and some of them were still waiting without changing their covenant in the least until the last (33:23). That God grants the reward to the men of truth for their truth and punishes the hypocrites if He will or accepts the repentance. Verily, God is The Most Forgiver Most Merciful (33:24). And God shoves the pagans (kafaroo) away with their rage they get nothing while God provides the victory to the believers. God is The Most Powerful Most Honorable" **(33:25).**

5. Hodaebiyah Truce

In the pilgrimage period of 628 AD, Mohammad and his 1,000 companions went to Mecca to meet the terms of the fifth pillar of Islam; they did not bring the weapon. At the village of Hodaebiyah a couple miles before Mecca they took a rest and discussed what to do. The months of *Zolqa'dah* and *Zolhijjah* in which they were going to fulfill the pilgrimage were sacred months and absolutely no war allowed; this tradition applied since the era of Abraham. But, just in case the Meccans broke the tradition, Mohammad sent Osman bin Affan to go to Mecca to investigate the stance of Meccans.

The aroma of enmity still stood after three consecutive wars between the Meccans and the Moslems i.e. Badr, Ohod and Confederates wars and it was not a perfect time to enter the city of enemy. Osman bin Affan was a brave companion, otherwise he never entered Mecca alone, and as he entered Mecca he was detained, during the interrogation he said he and another companions are going to fulfill the obligation to visit Ka'bah.

144

The Meccan leaders let Osman to do what he needed but he declined because he wanted all Moslems to do the Hajj. The negotiation between Osman and the Meccans extended for a couple days, and because Osman did not come back to Hodaebiyah and no news from or about him then the waiting Moslems in Hodaebiyah were anxious about his safety especially after the spread of rumor that Osman was killed. The Moslems established the short assembly and made the pledge to fight the Meccans if Osman was killed; this pledge was later named the *Bae'atur-Ridwan* or The Pledge of Readiness.

A day later Osman came back and told what happened, and the next day *Suhail bin Amroh* a Quraysh envoy came to Hodaebiyah to negotiate the truce. The both parties reached an agreement on the subjects of:

(1) The both parties would not fight each other for ten years

(2) The Moslems cancelled their intention to visit Ka'bah in this year and would do it next year

(3) Any people sought the refuge from Medina to Mecca, he or she would **not** sent back to Medina, but any people sought the refuge from Mecca to Medina he or she **had to** be sent back to Mecca.

The truce -especially in the third point- seemed to politically undermine the Moslems settled in Medina even after the *de facto* victory of Confederate War; that was the way some companions thought. Omar bin Khattab the prominent companion abruptly expressed his complaint over this third point.

Later on, Mohammad explained why he accepted the third point. If a Moslem sought the refuge and went from Medina to Mecca it was a clue that his/her faith was very weak and did not deserve to join the new society in Medina, he/she preferred to stay amongst the Mecca disbelievers rather than with Moslems in Medina.

Anyway, if a disbeliever came to Medina from Mecca he/she had to be sent back to Mecca because there was a possibility of a spy. It was the brilliant thought of Prophet Mohammad; the Hodaebiyah Truce has proved that Prophet Mohammad possessed the skill of diplomacy under the divine guidance (**53:4**).

6. Mo'tah

The Hodaebiyah Truce enabled Mohammad to consolidate the society and brought to him more time to spread Islam, he asked his companions to write the letters to the Roman and Persian Emperors and other rulers in the adjacent areas asking them to accept the ultimate truth. The letters were signed by Prophet Mohammad and sealed with a symbol of his ring indicating the authenticity; each letter started with a letterhead '*By the name of God the Most Beneficent the Most Merciful, This letter comes from Mohammad the Messenger of God*'.

The letters delivered by the special envoys and received by the addressee without incident, but when an envoy was delivering a letter to the leader of Ghassan tribe at Basrah, Iraq he was harshly rejected and as he went home a member of Ghassan tribe killed the envoy in 630 AD. This violation against the international diplomatic ethics ignited a war between the Moslems and the Roman ruler because Ghassan was under the Roman jurisdiction.

The power of 3,000 Moslem militias was not equal to 100,000 Roman warriors, the commander of Moslem army Zaed bin Haresah martyred along with Mohammad's cousin *Jafar bin Abu Taleb* and *Abdullah bin Rawahah*. Khalid bin Waled, a former commander of Mecca disbelievers -in the Confederates War and then converted to Islam- led the Moslem Army retreated from Mo'tah to Medina for consolidation.

In the same year before the wounds of Mo'tah War recovered, the Quraysh tribe assaulted Khoza'ah tribe an ally of Moslems. The assault was considered as a serious violation against the Hodaebiyah Truce therefore Mohammad prepared thousands of Moslems to restore the order, he ordered the Moslems to enter Mecca from every direction and to meet in one point, Ka'bah; it happened in the Conquest of Mecca.

7. The Conquest of Mecca

The Khuza'ah was a minor tribe settled in Mecca and its people tied the good relationship with the Moslem lived in Medina and therefore it was included in the Hodaebiyah Truce. When the Quraysh attacked the Khuza'ah, Mohammad prepared about 10,000 Moslems; he ordered the Moslems to enter Mecca from every direction to restore the order. The conquest of Mecca is also to insure that the fifth pillar of Islam should be practiced every year without any interference now and forever. The interference of the pilgrimage had happened a year earlier prior to Hodaebiyah Truce.

The huge amount of Moslem came from Medina made the Meccan so scary. The Moslems were ordered by Mohammad not to retaliate the past defeat of Ohod War nor another bitter experience such as the attempt to kill Mohammad and Abu Bakr or to retaliate the torture of Belal bin Rabbah by his master when he was a slave in Mecca. The conquest of Mecca in 630 AD was triggered by the Quraysh coalition to attack the Khuza'ah tribe the partner of the Moslems; this attack was considered as a violation on the Truce of Hodaebiyah signed by Moslems and the disbelievers in 6 H or 628 AD. As of the time Moslem entered the city no one was hurt and no single drop of blood was shed, the Moslems purge the Ka'bah and surrounding area from hundreds of idols, the truth came already and the evil vanished (**17:81**). Later on, this victorious conquest was recalled in Surah An-Nasr.

The conquest of Mecca was a perfect victory and the famous example how to treat the giving up enemy. When Mohammad and 10,000 Moslems entered Mecca, the group of Meccans who chased him when he was hiding in *Tsur* cave and the other pagans came around him like the death row inmates waiting for the last meal. He said: '*Do you know what kind of action I'll do for you?*' they replied: '*Mohammad, you are our brother and son of our brother*'. Mohammad said to them: '**You may go anywhere you want, you are free now!**'

This peaceful treatment soon spread in Mecca and the surrounding area, and the Meccans came to embrace Islam, a group after another. *When God assistance and the conquest of Mecca have come; and you see the people come to embrace Islam in crowds; so glorify God with the Praise to Him, surely He is The Most Forgiver* **(110:1-3).**

Mohammad was not a man of war-thirsty; he was unlike Joseph Stalin, Adolf Hitler, Mao Ze Dong, Pol Pot, Radovan Karadzic, Slobodan Milosevic, Haile Selasie or Soeharto who killed the defenseless people. If he was, he could do anything to the defenseless Mecca people in Ramadan 10, 8 H/630 AD and if he did so his teachings would be extinct before he passed way. So many bloodthirsty men died and their legacy vanished even before they die. It is not a surprise when Michael Hart positioned Mohammad in the first rank amongst 100 influencing people in the history of mankind. God praised his ethics in a short verse **"Verily, Mohammad; you are on an exalted moral values"** **(68:4).**

8. Honaen

The Hawazin and Tsaqef were two powerful tribes lived outside Mecca, they used to exercise in the martial art and they had had the kinship relation with the Meccan tribes. Therefore when the conquest of Mecca occurred, instead of accepting the reality they consolidated the power to strike the Moslems while they were still in Mecca area. Mohammad and his people only had the time of a couple days to face The Hawazin and Tsaqef; he was familiar enough with Hawazin tribe because he was amongst them a couple years during his childhood (see Chapter One: Mecca Before Islam).

Mohammad had have a praiseworthy habit to lead the army out of town to avoid the civilian casualties, and that what he did to deal with The Hawazin and Tsaqef.

In 630 AD, *Malek bin Aof An-Nasry* the leader of Hawazin tribe called his men and the members of *Tsaqef* tribe to prepare for a sudden strike and attack against the Moslems. He was a very smart leader and he asked everyone to bring along his relatives including the wife, children and the treasure as well. He knew how to address the public and to arouse the spirit of his people as well as to utilize the art of mass communication.

When the D-day came he stepped on a higher place addressing the people: "*O my beloved people of Hawazin and Tsaqef, today is the decisive one, you bring along everything you have. No way to turn your backs and no place to go home because your wives, your children and your treasure all are here. We are going to destroy the Moslems right now. Go ahead*".

By addressing the people to bring along their loved ones and belongings, An-Nasry in fact put the relatives of his people as the hostages and put the people under his absolute command.

An-Nasry arranged the hiding place for the women and children in a valley between the hills while he and his men were standing by on the strategic hill on the left and right side of the one and only way Mohammad would go through. When Mohammad and his men arrived, no doubt, they became the simple targets of a massive assault; even with a random attack on about 12,000 Moslems the casualties will be so many.

During a couple hours a few dozens of Moslems martyred and some of them fled and scattered to any place to get the shelter. After a moment Mohammad could consolidate his men and strikes back. Later on, this incident was narrated in Surah At-Taubah: *"Truly, God has granted you the victory on so many battlefields and on the day of Honaen War when you were so pride to your great number, but it benefited nothing to you, even you thought the earth was so narrow, then you turned back in flight"* **(9:25).**

In the other hand, God granted the victory and tranquility, He also sent the unseen Angel Army to punish the rebellious disbelievers: *"Then God sent down His tranquility to His Messenger and the believers, He also sent down the unseen angels; and punished the disbelievers (kafaroo). That is the recompense for the disbelievers (kaafirien)"* **(9:26).**

The Hawazin and Tsaqef fled to Taef district and defended themselves inside the forts; it was Mohammad's turn to put Taef under siege. After several days they gave up; they begged the safety of their relatives and properties and made a pledge to obey Mohammad. He granted without sentencing them to death unlike Qoraedhah tribe in Medina when the Moslem were under siege during the Confederates War (see Chapter Six: The Confederate War and Ethics of War).

9. Tabok

Mohammad was old and he was 60 when the Roman Kingdom considered the vast development of the Moslem society in Medina as a threat; and therefore tens of thousand warriors were sent to Arab peninsula. Nevertheless, Mohammad still led the Moslem to face the Roman Army; and as the habit he confronts the invaders out of town.

He knew the Roman Army was very skillful, and he tried to call his loyal companions and the prominent veterans to join this critical campaign. It was 9 H/631 AD a hard year for most Moslems because there were 7 previous wars within 7 years, the logistics and supplies were not available in the abundant quantity while it was the sunny days on the desert. On the other side it was the pleasure time for some companions when the time to harvest the dates has come. God criticized the Moslems who were reluctant to fight while the marauding disbelievers had come, it was a very polite criticism expressed in serial of the questions. *"O believers, what is the matter with you that when you are asked to march in the course of God you cling heavily to the earth? Are you pleased with the life of this world rather than the Hereafter? The happiness in the world is extremely tiny if compared with the Paradise in the Hereafter"* **(9:38)**.

Due to the difficult situation, Prophet Mohammad assigned the Moslem militia as "*Jaeshul-Usrah*" or the Army in Hardship but he successfully consolidated and mobilized his people to go to fight. He and his militias went far to the north almost to the border of Syria. The Roman Army never expected the enormous Moslems militia as they were looking at that day, and after a short fight they retreated. Mohammad and his men took a rest in the village of Tabok for 10 days before leaving for Medina.

Some hypocrites were asking the exempt from Mohammad not to go to fight because they were afraid of the temptation of Roman ladies. It looked like a good reason but God divulged their secret to Mohammad: "*And there was somebody amongst them who said: 'Mohammad, grant the exempt for me and do not force me to get involved in a temptation'. Surely they have fell into temptation (because he was a liar), and verily the Hellfire will be encircling the disbelievers*" **(9:49)**.

Three prominent companions Ka'ab bin Malek, Helal bin Omayah and Murarah bin Rabe' missed the Tabok War with a various reason; they were persecuted for more than 40 days and they felt so sad to miss the important event; later on God forgave them and accepted their repentance **(9:117-119)**. They were the heroes in the previous wars of Badr, Ohod and Confederates.

In the next year some tribe leaders came to him to make the pledge especially after the peaceful Conquest of Mecca. In 632 AD he attended the major pilgrimage in Mecca; at Uranah valley of Mount Arafah he addressed the people:

> "O my People may I have your attention, please. For I know not whether after this year I shall ever be amongst you again. Therefore listen to what I am saying to you very carefully and take these words to those who could not be present here today.
>
> O People, just as you regard this month, this day, and this city as sacred, so regard the life and property of every Moslem as a sacred trust. Return the goods entrusted to you to their rightful owners. Hurt no one so that no one may hurt you. Remember that you will meet your Lord, and that indeed He will meticulously calculate your deeds. God has forbidden you to take usury; therefore all interest obligations shall henceforth be waived. Your capital, however, is yours to keep. You will neither inflict not suffer inequity. God has judged that there shall be no interest and that all interests due to Abbas bin Abdul Mutaleb shall henceforth be waived.

Every rights arising out of homicide in pre-Islamic days is therein waived and the first such right I waive is that arising from the murder of *Rabiah bin Haris*.

O people, the unbelievers indulge in tampering with the calendar in order to make something permissible which God has forbidden, and to forbid something which God had made it permissible. According to God, the months are twelve in number, four of them (including *Dzulhijjah*) are sacred and three of these are successive and one is *Rajab* occurs separately between the months of *Jomada* and *Shaban*.

Beware of Satan, for the safety of your religion. He has lost all hopes that he will ever be able to lead you astray in the big things and major sins, so beware of the small things; never follow him ever.

O People, it is true that you have certain rights with regard to your women, but they also have rights over you. Remember that you have taken them as your wives only under God trust and with His permission. If they abide by your rights then to them belong to the rights to be fed and clothed in kindness. Do treat your women well and be kind to them for they are your partners and committed helpers. And it is your rights that you do not make friends with anyone of whom you do not approve, as well as never to be unchaste and adultery.

O my people; listen to me in earnest, worship God, say your five daily prayers, fast during the month of Ramadan, and give your obligatory charity. Perform the pilgrimage if you can afford to.

All mankind is from Adam and Eve, an Arab has no superiority over non-Arab nor a non-Arab has any superiority over an Arab; also a white person has no superiority over black person nor does a black person have any superiority over white person. Learn that every Moslem is a brother to every Moslem and that the Moslem constitutes one brotherhood. Nothing shall be legitimate to a Moslem that belongs to a fellow Moslem unless it was given freely and willingly. Do not, therefore, do injustice to yourself.

Remember, one day you will appear alone before God and answer for your deeds. So beware, do not stray from the path of righteousness after I am gone.

O people, no prophet or apostle will come after me and no new faith will be born. Reason well, therefore, O people and understand words I convey to you. I leave behind me two things the Qor'an and my decree, if you follow these two you will never go astray for good.

All those who listen shall pass on my words to others again, and may the last ones understand my words better than who listen me directly. Be my witness O God; that I have conveyed your message to your people".

This inspiring speech was The Last Sermon a closing guidance for the mankind he addressed on the Last Pilgrimage on Zolhijjah 9, 10 H/632 AD. A couple months later, on 12 *Rabeul-awwal* 11 H corresponded to June 8, 632 he passed away, the mission accomplished.

10. Suicide Bombing and Hijacking

A popular meaning of suicide bombing is "to kill someone else along with himself with the explosive". Killing of himself is strictly forbidden as clearly mentioned in verse 195 of Surah Al-Baqarah.

Anas bin Nadr was absent from the first war i.e. Badr, he was so upset and came to the Prophet saying: 'If God gives me a second chance He will see how bravely I fight'. When the Moslems were defeated during the Ohod War and some of them turned their backs and fled, Anas bin Nadr said: 'I apologize to you for what they did, and now I go the war', he went to the battlefield and kept going to fight and did not care about the oncoming arrows and spears. In the battlefield Saad bin Moadz met him and said: 'O Saad bin Moadz, by the name of God I smell the aroma of Paradise'. Later on, Saad bin Moadz reported to Prophet Mohammad: 'I am not sure I can achieve what Anas bin Nadr did to fight the disbelievers; he was so courageous, I found he was mutilated, more than eighty wounds by sharp weapons were on his body. Nobody recognized him but his sister who recognized a sign on his finger' (authentic hadith certified by Bokhary). Bin Nadr nephew, Anas bin Malik who narrated this story said: 'We used to think that this verse was revealed honoring my uncle': *Amongst the believers there are the men who maintain their covenant to God, and some of them fulfilled the obligation as martyr, and some of them were still waiting without changing their covenant in the least until the last (33:23)*. Later, in the Confederates War Saad bin Moadz martyred to defend Medina from the invaders, at last he could emulate his friend Anas bin Nadr.

The story of Anas bin Nadr could not be used as the basis for suicide bombing or another kind of violence; there is a clear difference between the both. Anas bin Nadr did in the battlefield against the fighting army while suicide bombing and another kind of violence are in the populated municipal area to generate the public fear and chaos.

A popular meaning of hijacking is "to take over the control of any tool without authorization". To take over a tool without authorization is a theft, a theft is strictly forbidden in the Islamic law; and to kill the innocence people is the major sin.

The suicide bombing, hijacking, terror attack and *fitnah* are *haram* (forbidden and unlawful) because the victims are always the unrelated innocent people to the case the actors engaged on. It is free for anybody to reserve the different choice with his/her own responsibility, but the **jihad** should have not slipped away from lawful struggle to the violence and terror.

11. The Ethics of War

Since the ancient time the civilized people recognized the ethics of war except at the time of Pharaoh who tortured and punished his people by crucifixion and cutting a hand off and cutting a leg off for each defector.

Islam, since 1400 years ago has established the ethics of war, here some of them:

(1)   Do everything possible to stop the attacking pagans or any group who has a special purpose to wipe Islam out from any region at any cost, but as they surrender the Law of POW should be established.

Whenever there is any aggression against the Moslems with the intension to wipe Islam out or to give a hard time to practicing Islam, then it should be taken care seriously; and for every Moslem has an obligation as revealed in the legitimate verses, this is counter attack doctrine. "*And what the matter with you so do not fight in the cause of God while the disabled and oppressed people amongst the men, women and children were crying 'O Our Lord, please rescue us from this oppressor's town, and raise from You for us anyone who will guide and protect us' (4:75)*".

"If they cease then God is the Most Forgiving the Most Merciful (2:192). And fight them until there is no more 'fitnah' (bad conditions such as polytheism, chaos, etc.) and until the worship is for God merely; but if they cease then no transgressing but for the 'zalimoon' (the wrong doers or those who did the inappropriate deeds) **(2:193)."**

"The *sacred month is for the sacred month, and there is the Qesas (the equal punishment) for the prohibited actions; and whosoever to transgress the prohibition against you then do the equal action. Fear God, and know that God is by the side of the 'Muttaqeen' the pious person* **(2:194)."**

"And *fight them until there is no more fitnah (polytheism, chaos) and until the religion will be completely for God; and if they stop from worshipping other than God then certainly God will see what they do"* **(8:39).**

In another verse (**60:9**) there is a term of 'qaatalookom' or 'they **fought** you'; it is a past tense verb indicating the war has occurred and the attacking disbelievers started it. If the Moslems were attacked first then the war is obligatory, if any adult Moslem evaded his obligation to fight the attacking disbelievers then he will be punished. Mohammad provided the Moslems an example when Medina invaded by the Confederates. The reason of invasion is wipe Islam out and to destroy the Moslem society; they would be forced to leave Medina while the Qoraedhah tribe inside the city became accomplice to the Confederates. The verse 9 of Surah Al-Momtahenah perfectly depicted the situation during the attack of disbelievers in 627 AD: **"In** *fact, God forbids you from being friendly to people who fought you for the reason of your religion, and those who forced you to leave your homes and those who helped to force you to leave your homes. And whosoever will befriend them then they will be* **"the zalimoon"** *(wrongdoers, disobedient to God)"* **(60:9).**

(2)   If the Moslems are lured to fight during the sacred months, they should have not started the fight; but if the enemy is attacking first then they may forget the sacred months and go to fight. *And when the sacred months passed, then kill the polytheists whenever you find them, and capture them and besiege them and keep them under surveillance. But if they repent and perform the prayer and pay the obligatory charity then leave them free. God is Most Forgiver Most Merciful* **(9:5).**

This verse is also alerting the Moslems about the possibility of attack from the disbeliever taking the advantages from the idle situation during the sacred months that is the meaning of '**keep them under surveillance'.**

(3)   Treat the POW accordingly, no torture allowed, God promised a big reward in the Hereafter.

The main objective of war is to restore the order after the chaos. The fight is obligatory against the attacking disbelievers, but as they surrender or cease then the fight has to be terminated, and the prisoner of wars (POW) has to be treated accordingly with food, medication and shelter.

The special attention was awarded to the POW, Prophet Mohammad was ordered to take care of them and maintain their rights; this is the ethics of war in Islam.

God grants the big reward for the Moslems who take care of the POW: **"***And (the pious Moslems tell their story why God granted them to enter the Paradise because) they provided the food with love to the poor, orphan and prisoner of war. They said: 'We give you the food in the course of God; we never expect your reward or thankfulness'. 'Verily, we only fear from our Lord in the Day of Judgment where the people come with the horrible face and full with unresolved burden'***"** **(76:8-10).**

It is clear from this verse that the main objective of the war is **not** to kill the enemy as much as possible, otherwise the killing of POW is recommended and not necessary to take care of them. The main idea of the good treatment to the POW is to provide them a real example what the Islam is.

(4)   Grant the asylum for non-Moslem regardless of whether he/she will be embracing Islam or not.

And if anyone of the polytheists seeks your protection then grant him the asylum so he can hear the truth of God's verse and then escort him to the place he can be secure, that is because they are the fool people **(9:6).** This verse 6 of Surah At-Taobah is a guarantee of safety and security for anyone who seeks the asylum from the Moslems without considering his/her future faith; the main idea is the disbeliever will soon hear the truth of God's verse.

The attacking disbelievers are not understanding the divine truth otherwise they will not attack the Moslems, therefore if they are asking the refuge then grant the safety for them even without their promise to embrace Islam in the future. To embrace Islam is the guidance from God; it is His decision to enlighten their hearts.

(5)   Kill the defectors and the accomplice.

The detail of the punishment was concluded from the practice during Mohammad lifetime when some residents of Medina secretly helped the invader.

They (the hypocrites inside Medina) think that the Confederates have not yet withdrawn, and whenever the Confederates come back, they wish they were in the desert among the Bedouins watching about your conditions (news); and if they by your side they will not fight but a little **(33:20).**

They did not participate in defending the city; they hid somewhere and therefore did not know that the Confederates left Medina. During the dangerous situation within wartime where the Confederates put Medina under siege in 5 H/625 AD, the leader of Qoraedhah tribe *Kaab bin Asad* betrayed the Moslems and became an accomplice with Hoyai bin Akhtab the leader of Nadhir tribe. The Qoraedhah tribe was encouraged to cancel the coexistence agreement and suggested to collaborate the Confederates to destabilize the Moslems from inside the city of Medina.

Upon this betrayal, Prophet Mohammad sent his two companions Sa'ad bin Moadz the leader of Aus tribe and Sa'ad bin Obadah the leader of Khazraj tribe as the envoy to the Qoraedhah tribe to persuade them; but bin Moadz and bin Obadah were harshly rejected. Later, they would be requiring Sa'ad bin Moadz to help them.

When God sent the heavy rain and tornado so it was easy for the Moslems to destroy the Confederates, then the Qoraedhah tribe stood alone and retreated to their fortified home inside Medina. They were put under siege for 25 days; later on, God recalls this betrayal in Surah of The Confederates. "*And about (Qoraedhah tribe from) People of The Holy Scripture who collaborated the Confederates, God brought them down from their forts and hurled the fear into their hearts so it was easy to you to sentence them to death and to detain some of them (33:26). And God assigned you to takeover their lands, homes, treasures and farms which you never stepped on. God is The Most Powerful to do anything*" **(33:27)**.

After 25 days under siege, the Qoraedhah surrendered and asked for Sa'ad bin Moadz -the envoy they knew- to be a judge. After starting the legal proceeding bin Moadz came with a verdict: Not all members of Qoraedhah tribe would be killed. The women, children, and the elders were put in the temporary custody before set them free to make clear who was the spy; but the men who went to the war and collaborated the Confederates were sentenced to death. The Qoraedhah tribe accepted the verdict and did not appeal to the Prophet since Sa'ad bin Moadz's deliberation was based on the Torah and they knew it. The verdict of Sa'ad bin Moadz was so revolutionary and wise even if it will be compared to the Geneva Convention more than a dozen centuries later.

Later on, this famous war was narrated completely in Surah Al-Ahzaab from verse 9 to 27, one of them i.e. the verse 19 was articulated in the most strict language in the Qor'an ever since. "*They despaired to you, when the fear comes you see them looking at you with upside down eyes like unconscious person encountering a death but, when the fear disappears they smite you with the sharp tongues while they are tightfisted to do the good deeds. They are disbelievers (lam yo'minoo) and God makes their previous good deeds void; that is easy for God*" (33:19).

(6)   Comply with the truce; but if the other party disobeys then give them 4-month grace period to comply with the existing truce or declare the war.

This is God and His Messenger's declaration of the freedom from obligations to those of the polytheists, with whom you made a treaty (9:1). So you the polytheists may travel freely for four months throughout the land (to prepare the war), but for your information that you cannot defeat God; and God will disgrace the disbelievers (kaafiroon) (9:2).

There are two legal reasons to cancel a truce of 630 AD, God in 631 AD ordered Mohammad to cancel the existing truce because:

(a) Banu Nadhir a chaotic tribe in Medina established a new alliance with another tribes in Mecca and Medina to prepare another war, and

(b) They spread the disinformation in preparing the massive war to retaliate their eviction from Medina in 626 AD.

A four-month grace period is very essential and a long time to think; it is necessary as the final choice between complying with the truce or the war. This is one amongst the ethics of war in Islam.

(7) No eternal allies and no perpetual enemies.

Today's enemy may turn a good friend tomorrow, or vise versa. The one and only eternal value is to maintain the good relationship between all people based on the iman (faith) without discriminating the race, nationality, gender, wealth and religion (see Mohammad's last sermon). If a Moslem successfully emulates the exalted moral stance of Prophet Mohammad then one half of his personal obligation toward God is fulfilled.

There are some verses encouraging the Moslem to practice the good deeds, and how peaceful this doctrine is:

"Verily, Mohammad you are on exalted moral values (68:4). Perhaps God will create a friendship between you and a part of the group to whom you conduct the enmity. And God is the Most Powerful Most Forgiving Most Merciful (60:7), God does not forbid you to deal with and to be nice to the people who do not fight against you and who do not force you to leave your homes. Verily, God loves the wise people" **(60:8).**

Today the Moslems are far away from the era of Prophet Mohammad and his companions in which the examples and teachings were so fresh and clear. Even a couple years after Mohammad passed away where so many companions still alive, there was an incident of misunderstanding of a verse when Qodama was appointed as the governor of Bahrain under the administration of Omar bin Khattab. Qodamah was a hero in some battles so he was a prominent companion of Mohammad; but Jarod another companion has found Qodama was drunk. To drink the alcoholic beverage was forbidden by Islamic law; therefore Jarod reported the incident to Omar bin Khattab. Qodama was called to come to the capital where he was under investigation, he admitted to drink the alcoholic beverage and was drunk. As a defendant he defended himself by referring to a verse of Surah Al-Ma'edah verse 93 (see Chapter Four: Asbaabun-Nozool). Omar bin Khattab then asked if anybody to refute, and Abdulla bin Abbas did. He said: "The verse that Qodama was referring in fact is an excuse for those who passed away before the verse 90 of Surah Al-Ma'edah was revealed where all alcoholic beverages are forbidden therein. The Surah Al-Ma'edah verse 93 was revealed as the answer on the inquiry by some companions concerning Mohammad's uncle Hamza bin Abdul-Mutalib, he was a martyr but he and another martyrs used to consume the alcoholic beverage in the past, they were forgiven". By this explanation, Omar bin Khattab sentenced Qodama with the mandatory lash.

When prominent companions like Qodama who ever met face to face with Mohammad could be wrong, what about the Moslem today?

USA is too strong for the terrorists, united we stand. As NBC's Jay Leno said on July 22, 2002: "The terrorist cannot destroy America, but Wall Street can". He said this sarcasm after the collapse of Enron Inc with the multi-million dollars vanished, a biggest lost for the investors ever since and an incomparable financial scandal in the American history. His comment was issued before Bernie Madoff Ponzi scheme being exposed with investors lost 50 billion dollars.

It has been not easy to determine who the enemy of Islam is; the normative sources have to be deeply discussed in advance by *istinbaat*. The term of "enemy of Islam" should be unmistakably distinguished from "the enemy of government ruled by the Moslems". Each party in the war between Iran and Iraq (1980-1988) could not claim the other as "the enemy of Islam", the same case applies for both Iraq and Kuwait in the Gulf War (1990-1991) and Arab Spring since 2010 until now 2013 with no signs to recede, even the latest report per June 2013 the victims of Syrian uprising topped 93,000. The same case also applies when Indonesia invaded East Timor, just because Indonesia is *de facto* the most populous Moslem country in the world and its leaders are Moslems, Indonesia might not claim East Timor as "the enemy of Islam".

The Moslems should be wary to the claim or provocation using the term of "enemy of Islam" for the political objectives. The art of modern mass communication enables the using of sentimental or religious terms to inflame the chaos and terrorism.

Terrorism such as the September 11 attacks and Bali bloodbath and other incidents always left behind the unrelated and innocent people. Terrorism is always a cowardice action because there was no warning and no declaration prior to the incident; it is unlike the open war. The international society should have worked together to eliminate any form of the terrorism, either group-sponsored terrorism or state-sponsored terrorism, and to establish the international prosecution to search and prosecute the terrorists around the globe and bring them to justice. In any condition, the enmity or hatred cannot be used as the basis to perform the injustice or the violence. In any situation the impartiality and justice have to be established first: "*—and let not the enmity and hatred of others make you to perform the injustice*" (**5:8**). According to Islam to kill the innocence will considered as killing all mankind (**5:32**); every slain victim due to the injustice is equal to $1.61E+60$ people within 10,000 years. That is the Islamic doctrine in the injustice manslaughter; think it over before intending to murder anyone.

12. Closing Note

In most cases of terrorism, it's clear that the actors, either Moslems or non-Moslem, were young and energetic yet they did not understand their own religious teaching well. This objective condition has made them the easy prey for the religious predators and violence preachers who systematically sow the seed of hatred against the opposite group. Timothy McVeigh was a victim of violence preacher who indoctrinated him that the US government is absolutely wrong when it stormed David Koresh compound. McVeigh was not given an objective fact that David Koresh men killed four US Federal Agents in 1993. Rubin was a victim of violence preacher and twisted self understanding that Mosque should have been destroyed. The Mumbai terrorists most probably the victims of violence preacher that the Indian government was absolutely wrong in the demolition of Babri mosque in 1992; they were not given the objective fact that the Indian government was duped by the rally organizers who said they would obey the rules, however the Hindu extremists rally at the site of Babri mosque eventually erupted into mass killing with 2,000 deaths most of them were Indian Moslems. The Mumbai terrorists were not provided with the objective fact that the Indian government has nothing to do with the demolition of Babri mosque. The list will be very long to put all terrorist under the scrutiny. The popular example is Patricia Hearst, she was a newspaper heiress and a victim of kidnapping, yet she was indoctrinated by the kidnapper the Symbionese Liberation Army a terrorist group to be a member of bank robber in 1974; she was totally brainwashed victim; not the terrorist.

From Waco siege (1993), Oklahoma bombing (1995), 9/11/2001, plot to bomb a mosque in California (2001), Bali bombing (2002), Mumbai bombing (2008), Boston marathon bombing (2013), to London attack (20130 has taught us an important lesson that the actor always the young adult under 40 (with one exception for Rubin who was 57); most of them had the very radical thinking as a result of indoctrination and disinformation.

Their militancy was supported by the painful fact that hurt their pride; and at this point a good religious teaching might be twisted into hatred, and from hatred it could be incited into radicalism and from radicalism to terrorism.

The method to indoctrinate and twist the innocent young Moslems is varying; here is some of it. They were young, energetic, convert or Moslem born, radicalized and influenced by anonym indoctrinator or recruiter other than Imam of Mosque. They are 19 - 37; were not mature in Islam education background; they did **not** know the Islamic Jurisprudence well but following the religious leader without any doubt and question (blind *taqlid*). The pattern of violence since 1976, 1994 to 2013 is still the same: The anonymous recruiters influenced a group of young, energetic and innocent Moslems. The recruiter put them in a short training camp under the disguise of *free religious course*. This kind of course in Indonesia was named "*Pesantren Kilat*" or Express Religious Course. How to lure them? The recruiter came to a certain place and invite the neighborhood to join the free food; they assert that "the doomsday is getting closer and closer while we are neglecting our religious duty", then they take a note to enlist who wants to attend the free "*Pesantren Kilat*". Here, during the 2 – 3 weeks of course they were indoctrinated and radicalized. One the main doctrine is "*the pagans are filth, therefore they should be eliminated*"; they are presented the original verse of Qor'an with a twisted meaning "The polytheists are filthy since they consume pork: "*O the believers, verily the polytheists are filthy and impure (najs); so let them stay away from the Holy Mosque of Mecca and Medina (Masjid-Haramain) after this year. If you fear the poverty, God will make you rich with His bounty if He will, surely God the Most Know the Most Wise*" **(9:28).** The recruiter then twisted the meaning by adding the unofficial translation that the pagans should have been killed, while the original meaning is "**let them stay away from the Holy Mosques**", it's a prohibition for the non-Moslems to enter the city of Mecca and Medina and not an order to kill them; since the course instructors are eloquent to recite the Qor'an verse, then the indoctrinated students to blindly follow (*taqlid*).

Personally, I was asked to fix a 24 year-old broken girl. Her mother gives me a hard time to reeducate, de-radicalize and re-civilize this young lady. She has no burden to talk about the free sex wile it is big taboo in Indonesian community especially among the girls. She was subjected to multiple abuses including but not limited to rape; she was beautiful but totally broken.

Three week-course in "Pesantren Kilat" ends with the **Baiah** (pronounced **baa-ee-aah**, pledge) *to support the establishment of pure Islamic community by eliminating all "pagans" no matter if they are the member of the extended family. "Pagans", included the fellow Moslem who does not agree with their ideology and "religious mission".*

Our school in Indonesia has to fix the graduates of this course for a long time especially to de-radicalize them since a lot of them became insane or semi insane. We found two girls have been raped and suffered from the mental depression upon completion of the course. After a certain time they gradually confessed the method they were trained with, but the government authority did not respond to the public report, even later on we learned from the newspapers that the recruiters came from a certain institution and turned to have a special relation with the high level officials within Soeharto administration (http://revisi.joglosemar.co/berita/panji-gumilang-dalang-nii-42477.html). No wonder, the authority easily intercept "the plot to topple" the corrupt Soeharto administration, since the Soeharto special agent recruited the persons of interest or suspects who are defiant to the government policy especially to the "liberal religion" or "*aliran kepercayaan*" embraced by then-First Lady Tien Soeharto". As the recruited persons have no suspicion over who did recruit them, suddenly they were arrested for "plot to topple government". This weird and cowardice trick has been applied since 1976. The Indonesian Moslem majority in 1976 rejected the "liberal religion" but it was later officially approved in 1978 when the Senate of Republic of Indonesia (MPR-RI) approved "aliran kepercayaan" to be part of the official government policy (GBHN) based on the Decree of MPR Number IV/MPR/1978 (http://superkoran.info/?p=2125, http://www.tempo.co.id/ang/min/02/37/nas1_2.htm).

"Aliran kepercayaan" is traditional belief including animism (Arabic: *khorafat*) to believe the supernatural power outside any religious teaching; its follower does not necessarily embrace any religion. The majority of religious community in Indonesia; Moslems, Christians, Hindus, Buddhists, and Jewish are opposing "aliran kepercayaan", and the Moslems are the most consistent to rid it out from the official government decree as MPR's Number IV/MPR/1978 and its derivatives under the supervision of the Department of Interior. Anytime the Soeharto administration finds the people who denounce "aliran kepercayaan", soon they are labeled as "the public enemy who is trying to change the Constitution"; some of them were tried and sentenced, and some of them just kidnapped and disappeared. The loyalty of Soeharto to his wife Tien Soeharto had blinded him and led him to go astray. The Soeharto administration always name the advocacy group who challenge the "liberal religion" *"Gerakan Pengacau Keamanan"* (GPK, terrorist) but the actor intellectual never be caught; and then the authority would announce before the newspaper and TV journalists that "the **Islamic Jihad** plot had been thwarted, thanks to the community report". With this sophisticated method, **Imam Bantaqiyah** of Atjeh, **Warsidi** of Lampung, and **Amir Biki** of Priok Jakarta altogether with their students/followers were totally sprayed with the bullets, more than 1,500 died. Everybody is too scare to object, no national inquiry and no international inquest; a perfect Moslem mass murder. Anytime an advocacy group questioning the (past) effort of Soeharto administration to officially spread "aliran kepercayaan" and asking about the missing students who were kidnapped in 1997/1998, and then they are in trouble either kidnapped or killed by poison later as happened to **Munir**. The kidnappers who turned to be the elite members of Indonesian military special units have been put on trial and sentenced by the military tribunal (http://id.wikipedia.org/wiki/Penculikan_aktivis_1997/1998), but only several of them and not all of them; even the former high level Soeharto's military officials were and are running for president in order to make sure they are free from prosecution in this world, only.

Soeharto should have been brought to International Criminal Court in The Hague for the Indonesian Moslems genocide. Now, it is not necessary since the unseen power takes care of him, the horrible thundering bang has come to his graveyard on the day of his burial. As for Tien Soeharto, the guard of her tomb keeps changing; every month or two her guard resigns and due to replace and resigns over and over. The ex-tomb guards have the same reason, at night they heard a woman crying from inside the tomb (http://groups.yahoo.com/group/bhinneka/message/2286). This eternal torment should have discouraged those who abuse Moslems, and the Moslems who twisted Islam for political and monetary gain, and those who indoctrinated young Moslems in any part of the world to be radical and manipulated **jihad** into **terrorism**.

Appendix

The Name of Surah

No.	Surah	Revealed in	No.	Surah	Revealed in
1	Al-Fatihah	Mecca	30	Ar-Rome	Mecca
2	Al-Baqarah	Medina	31	Loqman	Mecca
3	Ali Imran	Medina	32	As-Sajdah	Mecca
4	An-Nisa	Madani	33	Al-Ahzab	Medina
5	Al-Maedah	Medina	34	Saba'	Mecca
6	Al-An'am	Mecca	35	Fatir	Mecca
7	Al-A'raf	Mecca	36	Yasin	Mecca
8	Al-Anfal	Medina	37	As-Saffat	Mecca
9	At-Taobah	Medina	38	Saad	Mecca
10	Yunus	Mecca	39	Az-Zomar	Mecca
11	Hood	Mecca	40	Ghafir	Mecca
12	Yusuf	Mecca	41	Fossilat	Mecca
13	Ar-Ra'd	Medina	42	Ash-Shoora	Mecca
14	Ibrahim	Mecca	43	Az-Zokhrof	Mecca
15	Al-Hijr	Mecca	44	Ad-Dokhan	Mecca
16	An-Nahl	Mecca	45	Al-Jathiyah	Mecca
17	Al-Isra'	Mecca	46	Al-Ahqaf	Mecca
18	Al-Kahf, Cave	Mecca	47	Mohammad	Medina
19	Maryam	Mecca	48	Al-Fath	Medina
20	Taha	Mecca	49	Al-Hojorat	Mecca
21	Al-Anbiya'	Mecca	50	Qaf	Mecca
22	Al-Hajj	Medina	51	Adh-Dhariyaat	Mecca
23	Al-Mo'minoon	Mecca	52	At-Toor	Mecca
24	An-Noor	Medina	53	An-Najm	Mecca
25	Al-Forqaan	Mecca	54	Al-Qamar	Mecca
26	Ash-Shoara'	Mecca	55	Ar-Rahmaan	Medina
27	An-Naml	Mecca	56	Al-Waqeah	Mecca
28	Al-Qasas	Mecca	57	Al-Hadid	Medina
29	Al-Ankabot	Mecca	58	Al-Mojadalah	Medina

No.	Surah	Revealed in	No.	Surah	Revealed in
59	Al-Hashr	Medina	88	Al-Ghaashiyah	Mecca
60	Al-Momtahenah	Medina	89	Al-Fajr	Mecca
61	As-Saff	Medina	90	Al-Balad	Mecca
62	Al-Jomoah	Medina	91	Ash-Shams	Mecca
63	Al-Monafeqoon	Medina	92	Al-Lael	Mecca
64	At-Taghaboon	Medina	93	Ad-Dhoha	Mecca
65	At-Talaq	Medina	94	Ash-Sharh	Mecca
66	At-Tahreem	Medina	95	At-Tien	Mecca
67	Al-Molk	Mecca	96	Al-'Alaq	Mecca
68	Al-Qalam	Mecca	97	Al-Qadr	Mecca
69	Al-Haaqqah	Mecca	98	Al-Bayyenah	Medina
70	Al-M'arij	Mecca	99	Az-Zalzalah	Medina
71	Noah	Mecca	100	Al-Aadeyaat	Mecca
72	Al-Jin	Mecca	101	Al-Qaare'ah	Mecca
73	Al-Mozammil	Mecca	102	At-Takaathor	Mecca
74	Al-Modaththir	Mecca	103	Al-'Asr	Mecca
75	Al-Qeyaamah	Mecca	104	Al-Homazah	Mecca
76	Al-Insaan	Medina	105	Al-Fiel	Mecca
77	Al-Morsalaat	Mecca	106	Quraysh	Mecca
78	An-Naba'	Mecca	107	Al-Maa'oon	Mecca
79	An-Naazeat	Mecca	108	Al-Kaothar	Mecca
80	Abasa	Mecca	109	Al-Kaaferoon	Mecca
81	At-Takweer	Mecca	110	An-Nsr	Medina
82	Al-Enfitaar	Mecca	111	Al-Masad	Mecca
83	Al-Motaffifeen	Mecca	112	Al-Ekhlaas	Mecca
84	Al-Insheqaaq	Mecca	113	Al-Falaq	Mecca
85	Al-Borooj	Mecca	114	An-Naas	Mecca
86	At-Taareq	Mecca			
87	Al-A'laa	Mecca			

Index

About the Author

Abdul Rahman Bahry wrote some books and magazine article in different subjects. He wrote *"Jadzab"* on TEMPO Magazine (tempointeraktif.com), Jakarta Indonesia, June 2000; *"Local Area Network"* ISBN 979.537.136.3, and *"Jihad: A Struggle or Terrorism?"* ISBN 978-0-9892988-2-7.

He speaks eloquent Arabic since he graduated in the Arabic Literature. He also holds master degree in the Political Science as well; he combines his expertise in Arabic Literature and political science in this book *"Jihad: A Struggle or Terrorism?"* which was initially published in 2003, 10 years later in July 2013 it is published in a special edition with up-to-date information specially about the Arab Spring, Mumbai and Boston bombing, and London Attack. His later book is *"John F. Kennedy's Nuclear War"* (May 2013), US Library of Congress Control Number: 2013902914, and ISBN 978-0-9892988-0-3. In this book he details the sophisticated trick to assassinate JFK 50 years ago.